IMAD'S

SYRIAN
KITCHEN

IMAD'S
SYRIAN
KITCHEN

**A LOVE LETTER FROM
DAMASCUS TO LONDON**

BY IMAD ALARNAB

HQ

FOUR

MAINS

136

FIVE

DESSERTS

200

SIX

DRINKS

236

IN SYRIA, THE SUMMER GOES ON for three months. It's always hot, every day. Blue skies and a perfect sun, you can count on it. I didn't pay attention to the weather when I lived in Syria, at all. Unless it was something special. But it was something special. It was so special. I realise that now. I didn't appreciate my bed until we had to shift from one place to another, sleeping on a two-seater couch or on the floor, or outside in the streets. But I appreciated it then. None of us fully appreciate what we have until it's taken away from us. We think it will stay like this forever, but I know now that it can all be lost.

In 2009, my biggest concern was where we would spend our next summer holiday. Or how we were going to celebrate my daughter's birthday, or where I was going to expand my restaurants to outside of Damascus. At that time, I ran three successful restaurants in Damascus, as well as juice bars and cafes around the city. I lived with my wife and three young daughters, with our family all around us. My children were doing well in school, we took trips to the countryside for picnics, we went to the cinema or out to dinner with friends, we celebrated marriages and graduations and promotions at work. We were happy. Things were entirely normal and there was no way I thought that would ever change. But then, of course, everything changed.

WHAT IS A REFUGEE?

My name is Imad Alarnab, and I was a refugee, an asylum seeker, a displaced person, an illegal immigrant. What does that make you think of? Be honest. Does it make you think of people deciding one day to leave their home country for a more exciting job or better opportunities elsewhere? Do you think of smugglers helping people enter other countries in the backs of lorries and on overcrowded boats in the middle of the night? Do you think of thousands of people crashing onto coastlines all around the world to take advantage of the citizens and governments there? I made that journey from Syria to the UK that you've all heard about – on foot, on trains, with false ID, crammed into the back of cars, sleeping outside afraid for my life – and I can tell you, we are all just like you. We didn't 'choose' to leave, it was not a decision any of us came to lightly. Every single one of us was forced. We had no choice. We fled our homes that we loved because we were no longer safe, or because our homes had been destroyed. Our families were in danger and we had to do what we could to keep them safe. What would you have done? We don't want to travel illegally. We don't want to take advantage of anything or anyone; we want to be part of a community, to work, to play our role in society again. We are all just like you.

On 27 July 2015 I hugged my family goodbye in Syria. Three months later I arrived in the UK, in October 2015. Leaving my wife and children behind, knowing the risks, was the hardest thing I've ever had to do. But I knew this was our only real chance at safety long term. My children were young, too young to make the journey with me; there were too many dangers ahead, too many unknowns. People often ask why I was intent on getting to the UK, why I wouldn't stop in Greece or Germany or somewhere else along the way. I had family in the UK, my sister, my aunt and cousins, and I spoke the language already. Learning a new language is hard when you are older, and you need to speak it well to be able to work, and I wanted to work, I've always worked hard. Getting to the UK would mean my family could join me, we could all be safe, together again. I was scared about what might happen to me, but imagining the future if we stayed in Syria was even more terrifying.

When I left Syria, my eldest daughter was very emotional. She was frightened for me, for herself and her sisters. She asked me to promise that we'd see each other within a year. And in that moment, I didn't know what else to do but to tell her 'yes', even though I wasn't sure how or if this was even remotely possible. I didn't really even believe it myself. But on 26 July 2016 – a year to the day since I'd last seen them – I was hugging my family again, this time in the arrivals hall at Heathrow Airport. It was a surreal, unbelievable moment. Surely some kind of miracle. And then, in December 2022, six years later, we were granted our UK citizenship.

The journey to get here has been long, and often painful – both physically and mentally. It has been fraught with anxiety and many, many obstacles. I have lost people close to me, and I miss so much about my old life. But I know that the life I used to have is gone now, it simply isn't there anymore, and hasn't been for a long time. I am so, so lucky to have been given a new life here in London. The people of the UK have welcomed me, and I feel at home once again.

I am so proud of what I have achieved here. I am so proud of Imad's Syrian Kitchen, and of all the support and love people show it and me and my food. I want my journey to be looked upon as positive and encouraging for others, to show what can be achieved. But I also want people to know that it has not been an easy one. It's not only my story; it's for all of us who have had to leave our homes, who have been scared, who have struggled, who have felt alone and abandoned at times. I want to share my story so that people understand what we have all been through to get to where we are today. It's been very difficult, but as well as all the hatred and violence, I have been shown so much love. Having lost all faith in everything, I regained my belief in people during my journey, and I want everyone to know that. I want my story to reach as many people as possible. With the support of good people, with an honest heart, you can achieve incredible things.

FROM A CARWASH TO CARNABY STREET

As unlikely as it may sound, it was as a refugee stranded in Calais for sixty-four days that I started to find myself again. It sounds hard to believe, but that was the point at which I began to rediscover hope. We'd been donated a small hotplate, and I was able to cook. We'd pick up leftover ingredients from local cafes or supermarkets and I'd make meals for as many as 400 people a day! It gave us all comfort, and for me it was a taste of home, a reminder of who I was. It reignited my passion, gave

me purpose – and it gave me the courage to believe that things could improve. Cooking brings people together; it unites us all. And with the help of so many generous people, I've been lucky to be able to explore my love of food again, to share it with others. Honestly, nothing brings me more happiness than seeing people enjoying food I have cooked for them.

When I first arrived in the UK, I found work illegally in a carwash, getting cars ready to be sold. I slept there too, as an overnight security guard. I hated it. I hate cars! But I needed to work, to support myself and my family in Syria. I was a good salesman, though, and when I could work legally, I had a brief career selling the used cars I used to clean. But even though I was good at it, it wasn't where my heart lay. I thought about working in a restaurant instead, but even though I didn't love working at the garage, I knew I couldn't work in someone else's kitchen, to be cooking someone else's food or giving away my recipes. I did try at the very beginning. I went for an interview, but instead of seeing me cook or asking me about my experience, the owner asked me to empty and clean his van, then told me I didn't look like a chef and let me go. I went back to his restaurant after my pop-up had been featured in the newspapers and I saw in his eyes that he regretted it!

All throughout my life, but especially on my journey from Syria's warzone to my home in the UK today, I've been blessed by meeting the most amazing people, guardian angels looking out for me when I've needed them the most. How I came to open Imad's Syrian Kitchen starts with one of those angels, a woman called Toni. Once my family had joined me in 2016, we moved to a rented house in High Wycombe where we lived for a year. Toni was very active in supporting local communities, including assisting refugees, and she'd heard about a project called Cook for Syria, which helped raise money for UNICEF's Children in Syria Fund. She came to me and said, 'I've been to your house, I've eaten your food, I know what you used to do back in Damascus. Would you like to be a part of Cook for Syria?' 'YES!' Of course, I did. So, in January 2017, she introduced me to another amazing woman called Layla Yarjani and within a few weeks she'd started inviting people to mine for dinner. She'd call me and say, 'There will be five people eating at your house in two days, will you be ready?' She introduced me to a PR company – who are still my PR company today – and from that moment on everything changed for me. Laila phoned me one day and asked 'What are you doing on 9 March? You're running a pop-up restaurant in east London.' Imad's Syrian Kitchen, the pop-up, ran for two weeks on Columbia Road, where the flower market is. All the ticketing and booking was organised, and the media contacted. A logo was designed. It was a dream come true.

The pop-up was supposed to be just a dinner each evening, but it was so popular that tickets sold out within 24 hours, and we ended up having two evening sittings and two Sunday lunches. I couldn't believe it. After that, I did pop-ups all over London, and catered for private dinners, weddings and parties, here and in Ibiza, Paris and Germany. But of course my ultimate dream was to have a permanent location, and in early 2020, Asma Khan – chef and owner of the Darjeeling Express, who had become a friend during this time – told me about an available space on Carnaby Street. And, so, on 19 May 2021, Imad's Syrian Kitchen, the restaurant, opened its doors.

Nothing will compare to the feeling of that moment, of course – it was everything to me. It meant I had roots, that I belonged somewhere again. But cooking on the steps of that church in Calais, where I'd slept night after night, was where it had really all begun. The first stage of my new life. To cook for people was enough to remind me that this was the right path for me, it was what I was meant to do. I want to cook my food and make people happy. I forever want to hear people say that this is the best falafel they have ever eaten!

And that's what this book is for: to share my story, but also to share my recipes that have meant so much to me. Like me, they have travelled and evolved, influenced by what they have been through, adjusted and changed, but always staying true to their beginnings. These are the recipes I love, they are for you to enjoy as though I am making them for you in your home.

OUR NEW BEGINNING

When my family first came to the UK, my youngest daughter was six years old. In the car from the airport, her first question to me was how many police barriers there were between here and home. Her second question was how many hours of electricity do we have in the UK? And her third was for how many hours do we have water? I don't want my children to forget any of these things. I want them to appreciate what they have now, to know how lucky they are. But I also don't want them to be emotionally affected by what they have been through. I want their experiences to be encouraging and to inspire them to reach high for what they want to achieve, to have the confidence to follow their passions and realise their dreams. I don't want what they have been through to go on affecting them in the way it still affects me sometimes today.

Often, I wake up with a start in the middle of the night and say to myself, 'Oh god, my mother will be so angry with me because I haven't spoken to her for so long!' and then I remember. When I heard she had died, I was living in a caravan on my own in west London. I had been in the UK for 50 days. I couldn't speak to her on the phone beforehand, or see her or go back to Syria to say goodbye. My Damascus died in 2012, and like my mother she'll never come back. I can dream about her, talk about her, think about her – but I'll never see her again in real life. And although I don't have closure over either my mother or my Damascus, I now have a new beginning for me, and for my family. I hope both my mother and my Damascus are looking down on me and are proud of me and of my daughters. I have fallen in love with London. London welcomed us in to be part of it, it made us feel at home, and I hope we will make London and the UK people proud too.

THE SYRIAN STORY SO FAR

In the winter of 2010 the Arab Spring began, first in Tunisia then elsewhere across the Middle East and North Africa. It was a long-awaited liberation for those countries, as their leaders who had held power, undemocratically for many years, were forced to step down by the demands of their people. A revolution was taking place and in 2011 fifteen Syrian schoolboys, inspired by what they were seeing abroad, spraypainted on the walls outside their classroom: 'The people want the fall of the regime'. They were referring to the more than forty-year presidency of the Assad family. A regime that took from its own people and promoted its acquaintances, and yet still continued to achieve nearly 100 per cent of the votes in 'elections', their unrelinquishing rule passed down from father to son. It was a regime that hung over us all, with growing unemployment and economic hardships felt by many across the country. It was time for a change, for Syrians to take back their power.

It started as a peaceful revolution by a group of idealistic students, but it was supported by the people. All we wanted was justice, democracy. We even naively thought Assad would be on our side, that he'd step down, following what had happened in Egypt and Yemen. We thought he would listen to us. We thought the whole thing would be over within a few weeks. Maybe a few months. Definitely no longer than a year. Instead, those schoolboys were arrested and brutally tortured, and protests began against their treatment by the police. And then Assad started to use military force to bring an end to the uprising. But unrest had now spread across the country, other groups taking up the cause, and by 2012 there was a full-blown war happening all around us.

It affected everyone. We have all seen things we cannot unsee, and that will stay with us forever. At first, they happened at a distance – friends of friends, distant cousins on the other side of the city being caught up in gunfire, being injured, being imprisoned. Being killed. But then it came closer and closer until there was no escaping. This was no longer happening to other people; it was happening to all of us.

No one would ever have believed we'd be where we are now, twelve years on, with the situation worse than ever, with fighting between groups that aren't even Syrian: Russia, Iran, al-Qaeda, Turkey, the USA – Syria has become a place for battles to be played out that have nothing to do with its own people, and it looks like it's going to go on for a long time yet with Assad's control even more extreme than before. All the people wanted was a voice. In a dictatorship, the people have no voice.

And now people are really, really scared. Friends have cut contact with me, blocked me on social media, because I have spoken out against Assad. The Syrian government, through the press, spread stories to divide the people, and they are now afraid for their lives for being a relative of or even for just knowing someone who says they are against Assad.

In January 2012, I was standing outside a mosque after prayers. People were shouting 'freedom, justice', but it was calm, no aggression. Then from out of nowhere Assad forces descended and started shooting randomly into the crowd. Just three metres away from me, I saw a boy, no more than 13 or 14 years old, get shot in the chest. He died right in front of me. I was so shocked and afraid, I couldn't even look at him. No one could say or do anything. I knew then that there would be no justice in this revolution. There would be no closure.

Everyone has a story like that to tell, more than one. We see them when we close our eyes. When we think of a 'home', that no longer exists for us.

Just a few weeks later, my eldest daughter was doing her homework in her bedroom. 'I'm studying' were almost like the magic words she could say if she wanted to be alone. It was the secret password that meant no one could disturb her. My wife called to her to come into the kitchen. 'I'm studying', came the reply. But this time my wife insisted and reluctantly my daughter joined her. Seconds later a bomb hit our apartment building. The whole side of the building where my daughter's bedroom was had been destroyed, with bricks and debris landing right on the bed where my daughter had been sitting. She would have been killed instantly. It's hard for me to think of that moment, even now. The shock, the relief, the fear of what could have been. The luck, the gratitude for whatever it was that made my wife persist. Even now we cannot talk about it together. We probably should, but it all feels too painful still.

We started shifting from one place to the next, as more and more areas became too dangerous to live in. Everyone's lives were now about survival, all while trying to hang on to as much normality as we could. But within just six days in 2012, all my businesses were destroyed and we had lost almost everything. But at least we were still alive.

In 2013, we were in a taxi, heading to another new apartment in a safer part of Damascus. We were almost there when I got out of the car and headed away, back into the centre of the city to look for work. I had been walking maybe five minutes when, from the exact direction in which the car with my family in had disappeared, I heard a huge explosion. It was an enormous bomb. Smoke and screaming came from where they were, and people were running away, terrified and crying. I found out later that 70 people had been killed. And in that moment, I was almost 100 per cent certain my family was dead. I ran against the crowds, towards where the bomb had fell, dropping to my knees when I found the car and saw that everyone was OK. They were SO lucky to be alive, I almost couldn't believe it. My wife hugged me close, down in the gutter, as we both took a moment to understand what had just happened. We then realised there were people that needed our help. The taxi driver took our children to safety, while we cleared the roads for the ambulances to get through and reached out to those around us in any way we could.

Around that time, I had a neighbour who worked for the Minister of Recollection, which was a department created by Assad to help end the revolution. (Its aim was to make it look as though people were coming together. Of course, in reality, it meant nothing.) And the Minister's security team was there too, helping in the aftermath of the bombing. After I had done all I thought I could do to help, I kissed my wife and began walking back into the city. On the way, I started noticing that people and policemen were shouting and pointing at me. They were shouting that *I* was the bomber. Because I had been seen running towards the bomb – towards my family – they thought I had been responsible.

The police grabbed me and started beating me right there in the street. No one did anything. They handcuffed me and drove me to Jisr-al Thawra (Revolution Bridge!), which is one of the most corrupt police districts in Damascus, under a bridge. I was so scared, I thought I was going to be killed. No one asked me anything, not even why I had run towards the explosion in the first place. The Syrian police aren't interested in the truth, they just want to find someone they can hold up to say 'they were responsible', so it looks like they've done their job. To execute someone. They kept beating me, so badly, kicking me, punching me, I was bleeding from my mouth. There was so much blood I was choking, so they turned me over, face down on the ground, and carried on. They were beating me so much that in that moment, I would have confessed just to make it stop. I would have confessed on TV if it meant this would end. That's how they operate.

But then the same security team who worked for the Minister came back: my neighbour. They shouted at the police that I wasn't the bomber, that I had helped rescue the injured, that they knew me, and that the Minister would be furious when he found out what had happened. I couldn't believe it; I had been saved. I often say that despite everything I've been through, I'm a really lucky person, and in that moment I believed it too.

I'm still suffering from what happened to me under that bridge, I feel the effects every day, in my body that won't let me try to forget, and in my mind.

KEY INGREDIENTS

These are the key ingredients to Syrian cooking. They are very helpful to have to hand in the store-cupboard.

Most of my pre-bought ingredients are Belazu. I find that Zaytoun do the best olive oil, za'atar and dates. There is an online resource for special kit named after a market in Damascus: www.ebay.co.uk/str/almaskiya. You can find unusual ingredients in specialist stores or online, but most of these ingredients are available in the supermarket.

CHICKPEAS

Always start with dried for the creamiest hummus, not tinned.

❖ ❖ ❖ ❖ ❖ ❖ ❖ ❖ ❖ ❖ ❖ ❖ ❖ ❖ ❖ ❖ ❖ ❖ ❖

DRIED MINT AND DRIED THYME

For drying mint, use fresh mint that is preferably not from a supermarket, as it will go black. A plant grown outside will be perfect – the stalks are much thicker and better to use when they are dried, whereas the thinner stalks are better used fresh. Traditionally it would be dried in the sun and then crushed with your hands.

Wash the herbs well and then hang them up as a bunch, upside down, in the sun to dry. If you can't dry them in the sun, hang them somewhere warm, but remember that they will be breathing the air so it's best not done in the kitchen, instead use fresh air if you can.

After 2–3 days, they will be dried and crisp. Starting from the bottom and working your way up the stalks, rub the bunch between your hands to remove the crisp leaves; discard the stalks as they'll be too tough and chewy.

Store the leaves in an airtight jar, where they will keep for 6 months, although the intensity of flavour will lessen over time.

My mother used to put the dried herbs through a sieve to divide them, putting the very soft and fine herbs in a different jar. Use the fine herbs in labneh, sprinkled over the top, or in a sandwich, or sprinkled over buttered toast. The tougher, larger ones are used in cooking – famously used in tabakh roho (page 181) – or to infuse olive oil.

PINE NUTS

Pine nuts are usually toasted before use until golden brown so they hold their texture and add extra flavour. Toast in a small dry pan or in a tray in the oven for 3–5 minutes at 180°C/Fan 160°C/gas 4.

❖ ❖ ❖ ❖ ❖ ❖ ❖ ❖ ❖ ❖ ❖ ❖ ❖ ❖ ❖ ❖ ❖ ❖ ❖

POMEGRANATE MOLASSES

It took me ages to find the right one – not too sweet, the right consistency, good flavour – I use Belazu.

❖ ❖ ❖ ❖ ❖ ❖ ❖ ❖ ❖ ❖ ❖ ❖ ❖ ❖ ❖ ❖ ❖ ❖ ❖

RICE

We use many different types of rice. When we are going to stuff things, we use a short-grain rice that in Syria we call Egyptian rice. For topping it with something, like we're going to do with the kabsa (page 166), I like basmati or American golden rice, which is a slightly longer grain.

❖ ❖ ❖ ❖ ❖ ❖ ❖ ❖ ❖ ❖ ❖ ❖ ❖ ❖ ❖ ❖ ❖ ❖ ❖

TAMARIND

You can buy this semi-dried in 200g packets – sometimes 400g. You can prep it all at once and keep in the fridge for up to 1 week, or just use as much as you need for the recipe. If you remember to do it the night before, brilliant – just soak it in water first.

Crumble a 75g dried block into a saucepan with 400ml water. Over a medium heat, bring it to the boil and boil it for at least 30 minutes to extract all the flavour and reduce the liquid. Strain through a sieve into a bowl; use a spoon to squash it through and scrape underneath into the bowl. You'll be left with just under 200ml and it will have a really intense flavour. If you end up with a bit less than this, that's fine – it's all about the flavour.

THE WAY WE EAT

In some cultures, you eat with your hands or scoop up your food with bread. In others, people use spoons or knives and forks. Across Asia, it's chopsticks. In Syria, and especially in Damascus, we use it all. You can do whatever you like, eat however you want, because eating is your own personal comfort zone. It is the centre of everything we do and there's no judgement, only enjoyment.

What is taken very seriously, though, are discussions about what you're going to eat next. It's a major topic! We never go anywhere without first deciding what food we will eat. Even going to the cinema involves planning snacks. We might take grilled potatoes or Syrian-style pizzas; smaller, thinner and crispier than Italian pizzas. After the film, it's definitely a sandwich, eaten right next to the sandwich kiosk you bought it from. You don't go and find a seat, you have to stand and eat it right there, straight from the hands of the chef. And, of course, there has to be dessert.

In Syria, the weekends run Friday to Saturday, and for many years we went to my grandmother's house for brunch every Friday. The whole family would be there, and Syrian families are big! Cousins, aunts, uncles – it was like a huge party every week, and it was wonderful. Syrian families live close to each other, no more than half an hour away, and I remember those get-togethers as feeling part of something bigger, of being connected. It was important. It was always noisy, there was dancing, there was usually something to celebrate and, of course, at the centre of it would be the food. There'd be a traditional fava bean salad served with pickles and yogurt, so delicious, dense and heavy, you needed a nap afterwards! You can find the recipe on page 198.

Now I'm living in the UK, our family time is on Sundays. We go on trips or just make time to spend with each other. And just like we used to do in Syria, we think about what food to take with us. It's never a sandwich bought from a service station, though! Can you imagine?! Damascus used to be surrounded by a beautiful countryside, with wide forests and rivers to explore, so much wildlife to enjoy. Of course, it's been ruined now by Assad, but before, we'd often head out there for the day or even to camp overnight. We'd buy fresh tomatoes, cucumber and parsley and we'd make a salad from scratch right there amongst nature. We'd fry summer vegetables: aubergines, cauliflowers, courgettes. We'd pick berries for dessert. And there'd be a barbecue: lamb skewers, lamb fillet, lamb fat, all grilled on an open fire. Maybe some chicken too: with shish taouk, or chicken thighs like on page 155. A whole day spent outside in the fresh air, with food as its focal point.

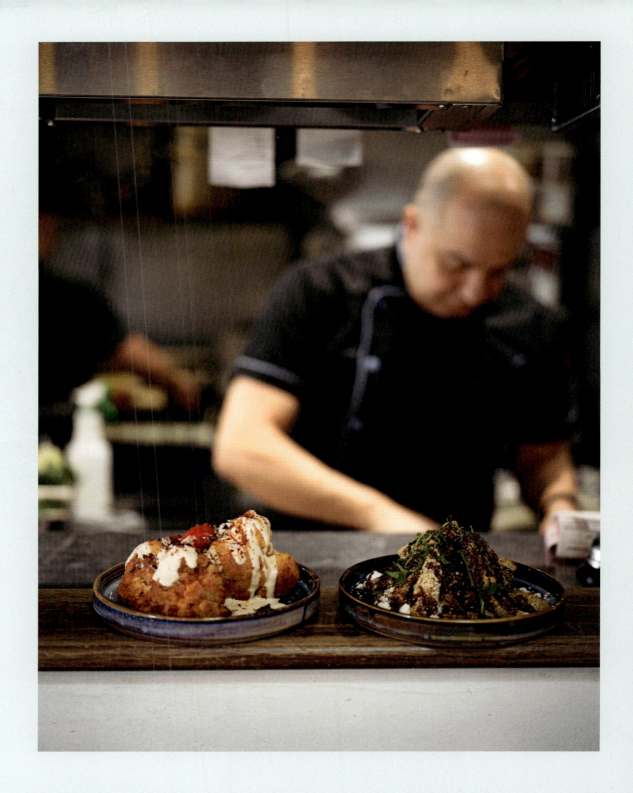

Every activity, every outing, has certain foods associated with them, and it's a huge and exciting part of the planning. Even a trip to the hammam involves the question, who's bringing the mojadara and pickles?! But eating out isn't how we usually eat. In Syrian culture, almost all of our meals are cooked and shared at home. Just like in the UK, though, it can be hard to get everyone together at the same time – with different schedules for work and school and other commitments – so most families try to eat at least one meal together each day, and traditionally it's lunch. Breakfast and dinner in Damascus are something light, maybe something with cheese or eggs. Dinner could be falafel or a sandwich eaten on the pitch after playing football. Lunch, though, is the main meal and there are always lots of plates on the table to share between everyone. To us, the idea of having just one plate of food is silly when there are so many textures and flavours to enjoy. We need more than one option!

In Syria, we say that the eye eats before the mouth, so even if it's a casual midweek meal, it needs to be colourful and well presented. There's always hummus and fresh breads, maybe a heavier meat dish or two, some vegetables or salads, pickles. There's always more than we can all eat in one sitting, so there's always leftovers. Those leftovers then go back in the fridge and become tomorrow's meals, along with some freshly made extras, maybe a new salad or a rice dish, something hot or a crunchy side. That's how we eat. We take what we already have and add to it, so even though we cook every night, it may only be a quick dish to supplement what's already there. And that is how the recipes in this book are meant to be enjoyed too. Make a few recipes, save what you don't eat for the next day and add to it with one or two new dishes. It's why we make hummus in such large batches, so there's always some in the fridge!

Syrians show their love through cooking and although we may keep our own family meals fairly simple, if you are a guest in a Syrian home you can expect something a whole lot more complicated. Spending three days preparing a meal is not unusual and symbolises just how important you are to the host. The more difficult the dish, the richer and heavier it is, the longer it takes, the more respect we are showing you. It drives me a bit mad! I'd rather spend proper time with my guests than be exhausted from cooking for days. But that's the Syrian way. My mother was very competitive about her cooking like this – she needed to be number one. If you happened to mention that someone else's cooking was nice, she'd then need to hear that hers was the best!

For us, there's no such thing as too much food. The recipe on page 117 makes a lot of falafel, but for Syrians, there's never more than you need. If you really can't eat all of what you have made, share some with your neighbours. In Damascus, we all lived closely together and this made us very sensitive to the people around us. If we're having a barbecue, we'd always send round a plate for our neighbours. And I do the same now

I live in Ickenham! If we're having lamb skewers, I'll share some over the fence – it's rude not to! And my neighbours now come round with whatever they have been cooking for me to try too – that's how I learned I loved gingerbread men!

I think one of the best things about Syrian food is that you can feel your way with it. You get to know the flavours you like, and you can make it your own. Of course, every Syrian thinks they know the correct way to make traditional dishes – and they definitely won't hold back in telling you. I honestly think it would make a Syrian unwell if they didn't give you their feedback about a dish! And that feedback is usually based around how their mother used to make it and why yours is wrong . . .

When I opened my first restaurant in Damascus, it was usual for a place to sell just one type of food – falafel or pizzas or burgers. But mine was bigger and we sold many different dishes. It gave me a chance to try something new. And then we opened a second and a third. I also ran a catering company, mostly cooking for non-Syrians on business in Damascus, which gave me the freedom and space to be even more experimental, as they didn't know what was traditional and what wasn't!

The recipes in this book are my recipes. They're mostly authentic, classic Syrian recipes, but in London I have the freedom to be a bit more creative, too. I'm not afraid to change things a little, and I've adjusted some of the recipes to suit how people in the UK like to eat. They might be a bit healthier or lighter, as well as coming up with entirely new dishes. For example, there's a dish called saroja on page 111. It's named after an area near where we lived in Damascus, which I loved and think of often, and this recipe reminds me of what it felt like to be in that place. Others are my mother's recipes that I've made my own, or they are the recipes I cooked along my journey to the UK that reminded me of who I was when I started to feel lost. It's food to bring people together.

So choose a few dishes you like the sound of and enjoy the process of creating a table of food, the Syrian way – really, anything goes! The dishes here are some of my favourites, but adapt them and do it your own way, and I can't wait to hear what you think.

ONE

SPICE
MIXES

SPICE MIXES

❖ DUKKAH 29   BAHARAT 32 ❖

KABSA SPICE MIX 32   RED TAOUK 33

❖ SHISH TAOUK 33   IMAD'S SAUCE 36 ❖

CORIANDER OIL 37   ORANGE-INFUSED OIL 37

SPICES

I THINK SPICES give different results depending on whether they are whole or ground. I prefer to use ready-ground spices and just mix them together, but if you want to grind your own, make sure you grind them very finely; I prefer to use a pestle and mortar rather than a spice grinder.

For all the mixes, combine the ingredients, transfer to an airtight container and you can store them for use for up to 6 months.

DUKKAH

Every family has their own recipe for dukka (literally 'smashed' in Arabic), so feel free to create your own version. I haven't added any nuts and seeds to this as I like to add them at the end when I'm ready to use it. The reason is that as spices are drier than the nuts they absorb the oil and moisture from the nuts so don't stay as crunchy and fresh.

MAKES 115G

50g cumin seeds
25g coriander seeds
10g pink peppercorns
20g Urfa chilli flakes
10g Aleppo chilli flakes

Toast the cumin and coriander seeds in a dry pan over a high heat, stirring them around, until a little bit of smoke comes off. Take off the heat and add the pink peppercorns to toast in the residual heat for 30 seconds. While still hot, use a pestle and mortar to grind them, then tip into a small bowl. Stir in the Urfa and Aleppo chilli flakes and, when cool, transfer to a jar and store for up to a month.

When you want to use the dukkah, toast any nuts and seeds you have to hand until golden (I like cashews and white sesame seeds), then crush with a pestle and mortar and add to the spice mix.

BAHARAT

Lebanese 7 spices

'Baharat' means mixed spices – seven spices. You can buy this ready made (or at a push you can substitute with garam masala) but if you want to make your own, here's how. It will keep in sealed jar for 6 months in a cool place.

Photographed on page 30.

MAKES A SMALL JAR

1 tablespoon ground black pepper
1 tablespoon ground cinnamon
1 tablespoon ground cardamom
1 tablespoon ground coriander
1 tablespoon ground cumin
½ tablespoon ground cloves
½ tablespoon ground nutmeg

Mix together all of the spices.

KABSA SPICE MIX

This is used a lot in Syrian cooking. It includes a lot of different spices but don't worry if you don't have them all. We use this spice mix but also use whole versions of these spices as they produce a different effect. It will keep in a sealed jar for 6 months in a cool place. You can buy this ready made if you don't want to make your own.

MAKES A SMALL JAR

1 tablespoon coriander seeds
1 tablespoon cumin seeds
1 tablespoon fennel seeds
1 tablespoon mustard seeds
1 dried black lime, ground
1 bay leaf, ground
1 tablespoon ground turmeric
1 tablespoon chilli powder
1 tablespoon ground black pepper
½ tablespoon ground cardamom
1 tablespoon ground galangal
1 tablespoon ground cinnamon
1 tablespoon ground ginger
1 tablespoon mild curry powder

Grind the whole spice seeds with the black lime and bay leaf using a pestle and mortar or fine blender, then combine with the ground spices.

RED TAOUK

This is a common spice mix that
is used in many Syrian dishes.

MAKES A SMALL JAR

1 teaspoon sea salt
2 tablespoons paprika
½ tablespoon citric acid
1 tablespoon ground white pepper
1 tablespoon ground ginger
1 tablespoon chilli powder
1 tablespoon ground cardamom

Mix together all of the spices.

SHISH TAOUK

You can buy this ready made,
but recommend making your own.

Photographed on page 31.

MAKES A SMALL JAR

1 tablespoon ground allspice
1 tablespoon ground cinnamon
1 teaspoon garlic powder
1 teaspoon ground nutmeg

Mix together all of the spices.

CONDIMENTS

IMAD'S SAUCE

Hot sauce

This is a great way to use up the last stray tomato in the salad drawer.

MAKES A SMALL JAR

1 large, really red beef tomato (or the best quality you have), roughly chopped
1 green pepper, deseeded and roughly chopped
Small handful of mint leaves
½ teaspoon ground cumin
Juice of ½ lemon
1 garlic clove, roughly chopped
1 small red chilli, roughly chopped
2 tablespoons good-quality extra virgin olive oil

Blitz everything together in a blender until smooth. Season to taste and serve with anything – for example, kippeh, hummus, falafel, etc.

Photographed on page 35.

CORIANDER OIL

Hot sauce

This will keep for up to 1 month.

MAKES 500ML

500ml good-quality extra virgin olive oil
10g cumin seeds
5 garlic cloves, minced (very, very finely chopped)
Large bunch of coriander (100g),
 including stems, chopped
Big pinch of salt

Add 1 tablespoon of the oil to a pan over a medium-high heat, then add the cumin seeds and cook until starting to pop. Add the garlic, coriander and salt then turn the heat off and add the remaining oil so that the coriander leaves stay bright green. Allow to cool then transfer to a container.

Photographed on page 34.

ORANGE-INFUSED OIL

This will keep for 3–4 months
in a cool, dark place.

MAKES 1 LITRE

3 large oranges
1 litre good-quality extra virgin olive oil

Pare the zest from the oranges using a swivel vegetable peeler, avoiding the white pith (if any comes off with the zest, slice it off with a knife).

Put the oil and pared zest in a heavy-based saucepan and bring to a very low simmer for 10 minutes. Be careful not to let the oil get too hot; we don't want to fry the orange zest – the trick is to make sure it isn't bubbling rapidly. If this starts to happen, remove from the heat for a minute to cool, then place back over the heat to continue.

Allow to cool, then remove the strips of zest and transfer to a jar.

Photographed on page 39.

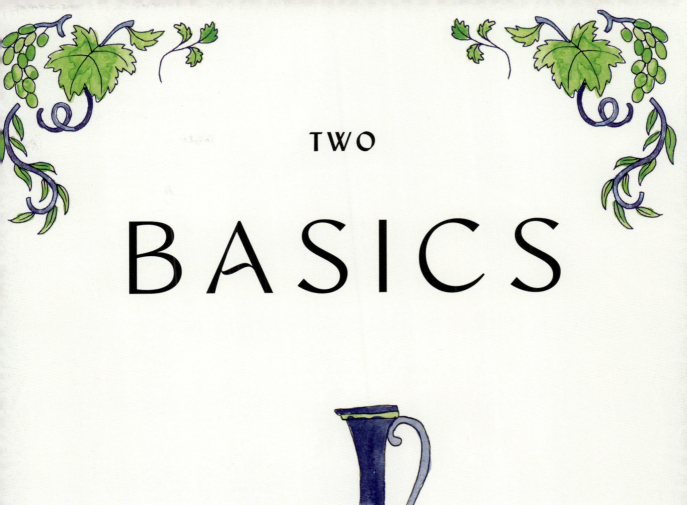

TWO

BASICS

BASICS

SAHAN KHUDRA

The green plate

There is something I love about Syria, which is 'sahan khudra' – the green plate. I cannot think of this recipe without fresh mint, sliced Turkish green peppers – from the north of Syria – derria, pickled cucumbers, radishes, fresh thyme, fresh lemon thyme, baby aubergine pickles, quartered small red onions. All of this can be used in the green plate. But you don't have to have it all at the same time.

One dish it goes especially well with is kebab Hindi on page 144; instead of using a knife and fork to eat it, you use pitta bread to scoop up the kebab and then eat with whatever you have from the green plate. Some people like to eat it with a slice of lemon, with the rind on. To go with kebab Hindi, I would choose cucumber pickles and green pepper, using the green peppers as you would your fork, to scoop it all up.

The green plate will change completely if it's for breakfast and the ingredients shown here are for cooked meals only. At breakfast we'd have fresh cucumber, tomato, mint, thyme and red onion, not green peppers or pickles.

HAWADIR

Ready things to present

In Syria, everyone is always ready to welcome guests at any time, and of course always with some food. In Damascus, we have something called hawadir, which means 'ready things'. So you have hawadir – jars of 2 or 3 types of olive, pickled aubergines, cheeses, cooked, sliced beetroot in garlic oil, breads and things to nibble on – to hand and ready to share at a moment's notice. In Syria, everything revolves around food and what you're eating next – even going to the cinema. If you're visiting your parents, the first thing they'll think about is what they're going to feed you. It was a huge problem if I went to my mother's house and I didn't eat something! We don't visit each other when we're fasting, we visit to break our fast.

TO MAKE

❖ ❖ ❖ ❖ ❖ ❖ ❖ ❖ ❖ ❖ ❖ ❖ ❖ ❖ ❖ ❖

Jars of 2 or 3 types of olives
Pickled aubergine soaked
  in olive oil
Cooked, sliced beetroot
  in garlic olive oil

You don't need all of these for your hawadir, but we'd always have a good selection of these knocking about at home ready for the doorbell to ring.

RIZ SHAEIRIA

Plain rice

In Syria there is nothing called plain rice, or plain anything! We always add something to everything. In some countries, plain rice is just plain boiled rice, but in Syria plain rice is a side dish to eat with a lot of things – kebabs (page 144), tabakh roho (page 181), jaj bailfurn (page 155), buttered halibut (page 170). We cook the rice with a very fine pasta, like angel hair pasta, and we always add spices. It would be too plain without it. We don't even consider salt and pepper seasoning; it's with everything. It's like waking up every morning. It's what you do next that's important.

TO MAKE

✧ ✧ ✧ ✧ ✧ ✧ ✧ ✧ ✧ ✧ ✧ ✧ ✧ ✧ ✧ ✧ ✧

200g long-grain easy-cook rice
25ml olive oil
½ teaspoon cumin seeds
50g (about a handful) angel hair pasta
½ teaspoon baharat (see page 32)
½ teaspoon ground black pepper
½ teaspoon salt
1 tablespoon ghee or olive oil

Wash the rice – always wash your rice. We have not even one recipe with sticky rice. We have a term – riz fal fal – which means that the lady of the house is very proud of their rice, with each grain separated from the others. To do this, the rice needs to be very clean and washed many times until the water is clear. Put your rice in a bowl and swish it through cold water, then drain it and wash it again two or three times. We do this for every recipe that uses rice.

Leave the rice to soak in the bowl of water until ready to cook, then drain.

Heat the olive oil in a saucepan over a high heat and cook the cumin seeds for about 30 seconds, until they change colour.

Keep stirring and add the pasta to cook for 3 – 5 minutes, until it has all turned the same golden brown. Turn down the heat slightly so the water doesn't splatter.

Add the drained rice on top and stir it once or twice – but not too much. Then add the baharat, pepper and salt. Mix, then pour in cold water until it comes 2cm above the rice. Turn the heat up and gently stir. Cook with a lid off for 2 minutes until the water is boiling, then turn down to the lowest heat and cook for 15 minutes with the lid on. Take off the heat and add the ghee or olive oil, then quickly put the lid back on and leave to rest for 5 – 10 minutes.

When you stir it through with a fork gently, it will be shiny and all the ladies will be bragging about the riz fal fal with all the grains separated and fluffy.

PLAIN BULGUR

Unlike rice, we don't wash bulgur – it is forbidden to wash bulgur! You just don't need to. Plain bulgur uses the same technique as plain rice but with more oil, as bulgur is a lot drier than rice.

TO MAKE

✤ ✤ ✤ ✤ ✤ ✤ ✤ ✤ ✤ ✤ ✤ ✤ ✤ ✤ ✤ ✤ ✤ ✤

50ml olive oil
½ teaspoon cumin seeds
50g (about a handful) angel
   hair pasta
200g bulgur wheat
½ teaspoon baharat (see page 32)
½ teaspoon black pepper
½ teaspoon salt
1 tablespoon ghee

Heat the olive oil in a medium saucepan over a high heat and cook the cumin seeds for about 30 seconds, until they change colour.

Keep stirring and add the pasta. Keep stirring and cook for 4 – 5 minutes, until it has all turned the same golden brown.

Add the bulgur on top and stir continuously for 3 minutes – you need to stir it more than you would rice as it is more likely to stick. Then stir in the baharat, pepper and salt. If at any point you think it's drying out, add a little more oil.

When you've mixed in the spices, remove the pan from the heat and pour in enough cold water to cover the bulgur by 4cm. The pan will be very hot so be careful it doesn't splutter up.

Gently stir together and bring to the boil, uncovered, then turn the heat down to very low and cook with the lid on for 15 minutes.

Take off the heat and remove the lid, then spoon in the ghee. Add the lid back on and leave for 5 minutes before fluffing up and serving.

SHATA

Chilli sauce

TO MAKE

❖ ❖ ❖ ❖ ❖ ❖ ❖ ❖ ❖ ❖ ❖ ❖ ❖ ❖ ❖ ❖ ❖ ❖ ❖ ❖

5 Scotch bonnet chillies
1 small red onion
3 tablespoons olive oil
1 tablespoon dried mint
2 garlic cloves, peeled
1 x 400g tin of tomatoes
½ tablespoon dried thyme
Large pinch of salt

Remove the stalks from the chillies. Peel and roughly chop the onion into 2cm chunks, or a similar size to the chillies.

Add the oil to a medium saucepan with the chillies and onions and fry over a medium heat for 15 – 20 minutes, stirring regularly, until they are soft.

Tip into a blender, add the dried mint, garlic, tinned tomatoes, thyme and salt, and blend until smooth.

Allow to cool then transfer to a container and store in the fridge for up to 7 days. If you want it to last longer, add a few tablespoons of olive oil to the top and seal tightly.

CONFIT GARLIC OIL

I serve this with everything, so use a good olive oil – the better the oil, the better it will taste.

I use this oil in my hummus as it gives it a sweet, mellow garlic flavour. You can also spread the soft garlic cloves on bread or toast with salt and pepper and chilli flakes as snack, or pour the oil and garlic cloves onto labneh for your mezze.

I always have a jar of this in the house so I make a lot here, but you can halve the quantities if you don't want to make as much.

TO MAKE

✧ ✧ ✧ ✧ ✧ ✧ ✧ ✧ ✧ ✧ ✧ ✧ ✧ ✧ ✧ ✧ ✧ ✧ ✧

4 whole garlic bulbs, cloves separated and peeled
400ml your best extra virgin olive oil

Add the garlic to a small saucepan with the olive oil (they must all be covered, so add more oil if necessary) and place over the lowest possible heat as you don't want the garlic oil to boil (never reaching over 100°C). Cook very slowly for 10–15 minutes until soft but without the cloves taking on any colour. If the oil starts to bubble, remove the pan from the heat to cool a little, then place it back on.

Remove from the heat and let it cool completely before transferring to a jar. If the garlic is completely submerged in the oil, this will keep for up to 8 months.

(Alternatively, you can add all the garlic cloves with the oil to a small, wide roasting tray, again making sure the oil covers the garlic, then place in the oven at 160°C/Fan 140°C/gas 3 for 30–40 minutes until completely soft.)

OPTIONAL EXTRAS

✧ ✧ ✧ ✧ ✧ ✧ ✧ ✧ ✧ ✧ ✧ ✧ ✧ ✧ ✧ ✧ ✧ ✧ ✧

Fresh thyme, rosemary or bay
Pared lemon zest

TAHINI SAUCE

We use this for everything – a garnish, dip, dressing; it's more like a seasoning for us.

MAKES ABOUT 200G

200g tahini
Juice of 1 lemon
2 garlic cloves, smashed to a pulp
1 teaspoon salt

Mix together all the ingredients using either a hand whisk or a blender on its lowest speed. It will be quite thick, so add iced water little by little until you have a smooth, creamy sauce. It will keep, covered, in the fridge for 5 days.

CRISPY ONIONS

These are a lovely addition to top so many meals and add some crunch.

MAKES ABOUT 180G

1 onion
250ml vegetable oil
Pinch of salt

Halve and very finely slice the onion, preferably using a mandoline, making sure the slices are all an even thickness so they cook at the same rate.

Heat the oil in a heavy-based saucepan and add the onion. Fry over a medium-high heat for 5–10 minutes until very lightly golden. The trick is to take them out a few seconds before they turn a deep golden, as they will carry on cooking for a few seconds after you remove them.

Lift them out, using a slotted spoon, onto some kitchen paper to absorb any excess oil, then allow to cool for a few minutes to crisp up.

If they are not crispy enough, you can add them to an oven tray lined with baking paper and toast in the oven for 5–10 minutes at 200°C/Fan 180°C/gas 6.

PICKLED CUCUMBERS AND CHILLIES

These purely sour pickles with no sugar, only salt, are very typical pickles from the Levant. It's really important to use the right salt here because the rock salt draws out the moisture slowly, keeping the vegetables crunchy. Table salt is too fine, and will pickle too quickly and ruin the vegetables, and using sea salt means they go soft and lose their crunch. If making in a different quantity, for every litre of water you'll need 2 tablespoons salt.

TO MAKE

✧ ✧ ✧ ✧ ✧ ✧ ✧ ✧ ✧ ✧ ✧ ✧ ✧ ✧ ✧ ✧ ✧ ✧ ✧ ✧

8 – 10 baby cucumbers
2 tablespoons rock salt
1 litre water
5 – 10 chillies
Peeled garlic cloves, as needed

Wash the cucumbers then slash 2 x 1cm vertical lines at the top and bottom of each, or any kind of slash, as this helps the pickling liquid to penetrate. Mix together the salt and water in a jug.

Place the cucumbers and chillies vertically in your chosen clear jar and press to fit in as many as you can. You want there to be as few gaps in the jar as possible; fill any large areas with garlic cloves.

Add the salty water until everything is completely covered, then close the jar very tightly with a lid. Put it in a dry, cool place out of the sun until the colour has changed from bright green to a muted pickle green. In summer this will take 10 – 15 days but in winter it can take 15 – 25 days.

MY DAMASCUS

Damascus is one of the oldest cities in the world. Parts of it are thought to have been inhabited for as long as 10,000 years. And yet, for me, it doesn't exist anymore. It has become a fantasy, a memory, a dream, a fictional place that even if it were possible for me to board a flight to return there in safety, it wouldn't be there to welcome me back. My Damascus died in 2012.

I wish I could show everyone what my Damascus is. The people there have a pure heart, they are so generous. It has a warm feeling everywhere, even the walls feel warm. Everything glows. The walls are alive, listening, watching over us. You can feel kindness radiating out of the brickwork. When you say 'hello', the people answer 'tafadal' – welcome – and they mean it. If they ask how you are, you can't answer 'I'm fine', you have to tell them really, what has happened since you were last in touch, how your family is, what they are doing. From your grandmother, this kind of detail is understandable, but these questions are from all your neighbours, the people you meet in the bakery, or when you're crossing the road. It can be a bit much! But we are also such an important part of each other's lives. We truly care about each other.

All Syrians are generous, but in Damascus they are very proud of their generosity. It makes our day if we make you smile. If you visited one of the markets, everyone would give you samples to taste, not because they want you to buy something, all they care about is making you happy and to hear 'Wow! This is delicious.' That's enough for them, there's no ulterior motive, no strategy.

In my neighbourhood, Al-Qasaa, people from all religions – Jewish, Christian, Muslim, both Shia and Sunni – live together in amazing harmony. We celebrated Christmas with our Christian neighbours! We all honoured each other's practices. Christian restaurants would paste newspaper over their windows during Muslim fasting times, and when Christians were fasting, we wouldn't have barbecues, so they couldn't smell delicious cooking over the walls. Ours was an especially mixed area, but all across the city we lived happily side by side, as we had for hundreds of years, and it was beautiful. Syrian men are family men, and we value our sons and daughters equally. Of course, you will always find macho men, but the respect we show to each other – to our elderly, to our women, how we care for one another – is something I love most about the Syrian people.

I've visited every big city in Syria, and most of the smaller ones, too. I've travelled from the border with Iraq to Turkey, from Lebanon to Jordan.

I love other cities in Syria, and have spent many beautiful times there – As-Suwayda and Al-Hasakah are high up there on my list of wonderful cities – but Damascus is my true love, my number one.

In Damascus, we deal with our food as though there is a love story between us. We use our hands to wrap our bread, and we take pride in preparing everything ourselves. Choosing to eat 'organic' isn't a thing because everything is always organic. You don't need to go anywhere special to get it because you can see it growing naturally. Until just a few years ago, no one bought milk in plastic cartons; you'd take your own bottles with you to the people selling the milk directly and you'd fill them up. You'd buy eggs straight from the farmer who kept the chickens. Your vegetables were bought seasonally, even if this meant buying 50 kilos of aubergines! And we'd freeze our own beans for the winter. We'd turn it into a family occasion. We'd gather round the table for a couple of hours with two big bowls in front of us: one full of beans to be podded and the other for the shiny green beans, carefully released from their pods. And then we'd eat green beans for a week and enjoy the rest months later when the snows fell. Fava beans, too. We'd chop our own tomatoes and store them in jars or in the freezer. Dried herbs as well, and spinach and another leafy green called mlukhea. It was a family ritual to pick the leaves from the stems and pack them into the freezer. All the families did this in Damascus. We all had a larder or pantry, with wooden shelves, kept in perfect cool conditions so that our stores would last all year. We'd keep cheese there, too. The cows would produce so much milk in the summer, after having their calves, so we'd make cheese by boiling the milk for a long time and then preserving it ourselves.

Unfortunately, people don't tend to do much of this now. They don't trust the electricity, which can go off at any moment for who knows how long, so everything in the freezer or cool room would be ruined. And if you google images of Damascus, instead of those warm, blushing walls, you'll see buildings painted white, red, green and black to show loyalty to Assad and the regime. Or just piles of rubble.

People often ask me if I miss Damascus, but it is Assad's Damascus now, not mine. There is electricity for one hour every twelve hours. There is no petrol or diesel for people to travel, or to run the school buses. Schools are closed for two weeks over the holidays, not three days like before. In Syria, the weekend is now Friday, Saturday and Sunday, and not because of any four-day relaxed working week! It's because the government cannot afford to fund the infrastructure, the transport network, the power to keep the office buildings running. But if you watch Syrian TV, they'll tell you life is good and Assad is great. They've been brainwashed or they're in denial, afraid for their lives. It's a broken country, a destroyed city.

It's been coming a long time, though, and maybe we were all in denial for too long. In my lifetime, we've never had any real ministers or elected government. That's not how it works in a dictatorship. In 1991, I had a car accident where a bus drove straight into me and I was in coma for 47 days. A medical police officer came to report on the accident and he told my family that the driver was now in jail. That there had been justice for what had happened to me. But then he recognised my uncle, who was also a doctor, and realised they had trained together. He said, 'I'm going to tell you the truth.' And the truth was that the driver was from the Soviet Union Embassy and he had returned to Russia the day after the accident, so no charges were brought against him. A free man. I'm still suffering from the effects of that car crash today. The revolution may have started in 2011 but the corruption has been going on far further into our history.

I can never go back. I am too afraid. I have been too outspoken against the regime, about Assad. There are Syrian army leaders on YouTube warning those who have left Syria not to return or else they will be killed. We are viewed as traitors. And I'm sure they are keeping track of what some of us are up to. When I had my pop-up in 2019, the Syrian media – Assad's propaganda machine – started talking about my empire of restaurants across Europe, achieved because I'd sold my soul to Western governments. They posted photos of me on social media. I didn't even have one restaurant! I wrote to them to ask why they were lying, but of course they didn't answer any of my messages.

Although I may not have any real closure on the death of my Damascus or my mother, I am lucky enough to have found a new beginning here in London – and I wish the same for Damascus too. I hope it will allow another young person, just like I was back then, to one day be able to have their own 'my Damascus'.

STARTERS, MEZZE & DIPS

STARTERS, MEZZE & DIPS

HUMMUS

This recipe makes a lot of hummus, but in Syria we like to always have hummus in the fridge. We make a big batch and eat it over 2–3 days at breakfast, lunch and dinner, and as a snack. We eat it all day with pitta bread – and it's also great with crisps and on the side of many dishes. There's pretty much nothing that hummus doesn't go with. It will keep, covered, in the fridge for up to 5 days, but if on day 4 you think it's lost a bit of its taste, you can lift it up with a little bit of tahini or cumin and it will be fresh again. If you don't want to make this much, feel free to halve all the quantities.

'Hummus' in Arabic literally means chickpeas, and it is a very traditional, simple recipe – carrot or beetroot hummus doesn't exist for us (and in my opinion shouldn't exist!). But what we do is add a lot of toppings – see page 70. The garnish is up to you, but the actual hummus itself is very simple. Although we are purists when it comes to hummus, I do have just a little twist in my recipe, to lift the flavours up.

I think one of the nicest things about making Syrian food is you can really feel it. There's nothing complicated in the recipes, so you can follow these or change them up and make them your own – it all depends on how you like them. I will give you a hint in these recipes, but I would love to see your creations using Syrian ingredients. It's not rocket science, you can feel your way – and feel love when you make them.

PREPARING THE CHICKPEAS

500g dried chickpeas
½ teaspoon bicarbonate of soda

First you need to soak and then cook the chickpeas; all hummus (chickpea) recipes start this way.

Put the chickpeas in a large bowl and cover with cold water to twice their depth, with space above the water, too, for the chickpeas to expand. Leave to soak overnight for at least 14 hours (but no more than 24, or the chickpeas will start to grow shoots), changing the water halfway through soaking.

Drain and rinse the chickpeas well then put them into a large saucepan. Cover with fresh cold water and bring to the boil. Boil for 10 minutes, then turn the heat down to a steady simmer. Now add the bicarbonate of soda – be very careful when you add it as it will froth up. The bicarb makes the chickpeas evenly tender all the way through with no hard centre, and also speeds up the cooking time.

How long you need to continue to boil the chickpeas depends on the kind of chickpeas you are using. If you are using Mexican chickpeas, start checking on them at around 1 hour to 1 hour 15 minutes. To test, take a chickpea and smash it with your fingers: when ready, it should be really, really soft. This could take up to 2 hours.

FOR THE HUMMUS

2 tablespoons ground cumin
1 tablespoon salt
3 tablespoons lemon juice
160g tahini
150ml water with 4 cubes
  of ice added

If you like your hummus very smooth and creamy, you need to blend it while it's hot. I personally like it with some texture, so I drain the chickpeas, chill them in the fridge until cold, then start the blending process. You will now have approximately 1kg cooked, drained chickpeas.

FOR THE GARLIC OIL

6 garlic cloves, peeled
100ml olive oil

Meanwhile, put the garlic cloves in a small saucepan and cover with the olive oil. Bring up to a low simmer then turn down and cook for 5 minutes until the garlic is a little bit brown and soft. Drain the garlic from the oil, reserving the oil and garlic separately.

Put the chickpeas, 4 of the soft garlic cloves, the cumin, salt and lemon juice in a food processor and start blending. Still with the processor running, add the tahini – this will make it thicken up, so immediately add as much of the iced water as needed to achieve the consistency you like. I prefer to keep it a little bit liquid because when you put it in the fridge it will thicken up a bit by the next day.

Serve with a drizzle of the reserved garlic oil, and the remaining 2 soft garlic cloves.

TOPPINGS

BOILED CHICKPEAS, SPRING ONION, CHILLI FLAKES AND PARSLEY

✦ ✦ ✦ ✦ ✦ ✦

Keep back a handful of the boiled chickpeas and toss them in a little of the garlic oil along with a pinch of red chilli flakes, a squeeze of lemon juice, a pinch of salt, 1 chopped spring onion and 1 tablespoon chopped parsley. Spoon your hummus onto a dish then scatter over the dressed chickpeas.

GARLIC OIL AND SUMAC

✦ ✦ ✦ ✦ ✦ ✦

You can use the garlic olive oil as it is, drizzled on top of the hummus, but at the restaurant we like to sprinkle a pinch of sumac on top, too.

SUMAC AND URFA

✦ ✦ ✦ ✦ ✦ ✦

Add a pinch each of sumac and Urfa chilli flakes to the garlic oil with a squeeze of lemon juice. Mix together to make a dressing and drizzle over the top of the hummus.

HUMMUS BIL ZAYT

If you don't have time to soak and boil your own chickpeas for this, you can use 500g drained jarred ones, which are a lot softer than tinned ones. Simply reheat them in some boiling water for a few minutes. Use tomatoes that are seasonal – cherry tomatoes, beef tomatoes, whatever is tasty at the time. Vine tomatoes are great.

250g dried chickpeas
Juice of 1 lemon
2 garlic cloves, smashed
  to a pulp or grated
1 teaspoon salt
1 tablespoon dukkah (page 29)
Bunch of parsley, chopped
2 spring onions, chopped
2 medium tomatoes, diced
100ml confit garlic oil
  (ideally; page 53) or extra
  virgin olive oil

Cook the chickpeas as directed on page 68.

In a small bowl, mix together the lemon juice, garlic, salt and dukkah.

Put the drained chickpeas in a bowl while they are still hot, and toss through the lemon and garlic mixture. Top with the parsley, spring onions and tomatoes, and drizzle over the oil.

This also makes a really nice topping for hummus, if you have any left over.

VARIATION

HUMMUS BALEVAL (CHICKPEAS WITH YOGURT)

This is how my wife likes it. Mix together the lemon juice, garlic, salt and dukkah as above. Then mix 3 tablespoons Greek yogurt with 50g tahini, and add this to the chickpeas. Top with the parsley, spring onions, tomatoes and drizzle of oil.

HUMMUS BELLAHMA

There are many, many toppings for hummus in Damascus but this is the most famous.

2 tablespoons ghee
1 onion, finely diced
200g minced lamb
1 teaspoon baharat (page 32)
50g toasted pine nuts
200g hummus (page 68)
Pinch of sumac
Small handful of parsley leaves
Salt and ground black pepper

Heat the ghee in a frying pan, add the onion and fry until slightly softened, then add the minced lamb and baharat, with salt and pepper to taste. Cook, stirring, until the meat is soft and cooked through but not crispy, then add the pine nuts.

Spread the hummus out on a dish and tip the meat mixture over the hummus. Sprinkle over the sumac and parsley leaves and serve.

YLANGY

Vine leaves

This dish is great for any vegan friends you might be feeding. You can find vine leaves in jars in supermarkets. They will be rolled on top of each other but you can simply unroll them. Drain the vine leaves from the liquid and cut off the stems, then lay them out. If you have fresh vine leaves that is obviously better. You need to trim the stem, then dip them in boiling water that has a teaspoon of salt added. This makes them a little softer and easier to roll out.

FOR THE STUFFED VINE LEAVES

✧ ✧

200g short-grain Egyptian rice
2 large beef or vine tomatoes, very finely diced
1 red onion, very finely diced
1 tablespoon dried mint
2 teaspoons ground cumin
1 teaspoon baharat (page 32)
50ml olive oil
50 vine leaves (see introduction)

For the filling, wash the rice until the water runs clear then add to a bowl with the tomatoes, red onion, dried mint, cumin, baharat, olive oil and a good pinch each of salt and black pepper, then mix thoroughly.

Prepare your vine leaves (see introduction) then lay one out, ideally on a tray, in front of you. Spoon 1 tablespoon of the rice mixture into the middle of the leaf. Fold the sides inwards like an envelope, then roll away from you, making a neat little roll. Set aside on another tray and continue with the rest until you have used all the leaves and filling.

FOR THE SAUCE

✧ ✧

Juice of 4 lemons
500ml water
1 tablespoon tomato purée
5 garlic cloves, smashed into a paste
1 teaspoon ground black pepper
1 teaspoon baharat (page 32)
4 tablespoons pomegranate molasses

Add the lemon juice and water to another bowl, then stir in the tomato purée, garlic, black pepper, baharat, pomegranate molasses and 2 teaspoons of salt, and mix together until combined.

TO ASSEMBLE

✧ ✧ ✧ ✧ ✧ ✧ ✧ ✧ ✧ ✧ ✧ ✧ ✧ ✧ ✧ ✧ ✧ ✧ ✧

2 starchy potatoes, peeled
  and cut into 1cm slices
Salt and ground black pepper

In a wide, heavy-based pot or flameproof casserole, 30–35cm diameter, layer the sliced potatoes to completely cover the base. Now stack the stuffed vine leaves neatly and tightly around the edges of the pot until you have used them all and have no big gaps.

Place a weight on top of everything. I have a traditional weight that is meant for this dish, but if you don't, then stack 3–5 plates on top instead, which works fine.

Pour over the sauce to cover everything; you might not need all of it, so just set aside the rest in case you need to top up later. Tightly cover with foil or a lid then place over a high heat until the liquid is boiling. Boil for 10 minutes then turn the heat to low and simmer for 1 hour.

Remove the lid and allow to cool completely, then serve as a side or main.

SAWDA

Lamb's liver

FOR THE LIVER

✧ ✧ ✧ ✧ ✧ ✧ ✧ ✧ ✧ ✧ ✧ ✧ ✧ ✧ ✧ ✧ ✧ ✧

500g lamb's liver, cleaned
  (and trimmed if necessary)
4 garlic cloves, peeled
1 green chilli
2 tablespoons olive oil
1 tablespoon dukkah (page 29)
100ml vegetable oil
1 red onion, thinly sliced
1 green pepper, deseeded and
  thinly sliced
½ lemon

Slice the liver lengthways into long slices 1cm thick.

Smash together the garlic, chilli, olive oil and dukkah using a pestle and mortar until you have a paste, then add half of this to the lamb liver in a bowl. Leave to marinate for 1 hour.

Heat the vegetable oil in a wok or frying pan over a high heat. Once the oil is hot, add the liver and stir immediately. Keep stirring for 5–6 minutes until cooked through and golden. Now add the red onion and green pepper and stir to cook for 2 minutes. Drain off the excess oil/liquid then add the remaining half of the garlic and dukkah paste. Mix together then serve scooped up in flatbreads or pitta, with tahini, parsley, pickles and a squeeze of lemon juice.

TO SERVE

✧ ✧ ✧ ✧ ✧ ✧ ✧ ✧ ✧ ✧ ✧ ✧ ✧ ✧ ✧ ✧ ✧

Flatbreads or pitta bread
2–3 tablespoons tahini
Small handful of parsley
Pickled cucumbers (page 56)
½ lemon, for squeezing over

FAMILY

FOR SYRIANS, family is a big deal – and it's also very big! My father was one of 14 brothers and sisters and the last time anyone counted, we had 98 immediate cousins. Whenever we all got together, it was always noisy, chaotic and lots of fun. My family is so extended that it's actually almost impossible to keep track of everyone, especially now with so many having left Syria, dispersed around the world. Last year, a delivery guy came to the restaurant to drop off a package. He told me he was also Syrian, from Damascus, and that he had left with his parents to escape Assad. While we chatted about our shared experiences, he happened to mention his family name and we soon discovered that we were cousins! And not even distant cousins; his mother was my aunt. This is how vast and widespread Syrian families are, and also how we can never escape each other for long!

Family is a very important part of Syrian culture, maybe even more important than the food we eat! Before the war when so many of us fled the country, we lived close to each other, almost next door. And we made seeing each other and spending time together a priority. I'd see my mother several times a week, and I'd ring her every day if I didn't see her. Syrians respect their elders. It's not from a sense of duty, we just genuinely want to look after those generations that have struggled through before us, that have given us so much. And it's not just those we are related to, either, we call all those older than us Uncle or Auntie as a sign of our affection. Never Mr, as that would be too formal, it'd actually be impolite. My daughters call my neighbour here Uncle David!

Now we're living in the UK, of course it's harder to stay in touch with everyone and to maintain those relationships as much as we'd all like. We have our phones and Facebook, but it's dangerous for those still in Syria to be in contact with me, so they try to keep their distance. It's sad, but I don't blame them at all. Fear of the regime is everywhere and you cannot be too careful. If I even sent money to them, even just $50, they could end up in jail. It's illegal to receive foreign currency and the authorities would see it as showing loyalty to ISIS. They're just looking for reasons to arrest you, or make you disappear.

Living in the UK means my direct family around me is much smaller. My sister and her family live in Doncaster, and my dad mostly lives with them too. We see them as often as we can, but most of the time it's just me, my wife and my three daughters. To me, my daughters are my everything. They are my greatest achievement, the light of my life. I wake up every day for them. If I hear the sound of them laughing, or if one of them hugs me or tells me they like something I have cooked for them, it feels like I don't need anything else in the world. Dana, Lana and Mariam; I honestly can't describe how much I love them. They are the most incredible, intelligent and well-behaved young women – but I really don't care if they are good or not. After all we've been through, all I want is for them to be happy. I know now that nothing is ever certain, you can't trust anything to stay the same. Our happiness when we are together as a family is our constant now. That is all that matters.

People say I talk about my daughters too much, but one of the reasons I love them so much is because they are my wife's daughters. Batool: absolutely, my better half. The love of my life who calms me down, supports me, keeps me going when I feel lost. There are hundreds of reasons why I love her, she is the most amazing woman. We have been married for more than twenty years, but I feel just as young as we were back then when we're together. My mother introduced us. She invited me to a family gathering and I had the feeling she was going to try to hook me up with someone there. I wasn't interested. I wanted to find a partner by myself, not be introduced to one of my aunt's friends! I went to the party entirely to prove her wrong and was set on not liking this person at all. But the minute I saw Batool, I knew that I had lost whatever game I was trying to play. I swear, I knew it in that instant. It felt as though we'd known each other forever. We were so relaxed with each other, as though we were already married. It was an incredibly strange and new feeling.

Of course, one of the reasons I love to cook is because it connects me to all this. All these memories, all that history, that culture, of my family, of the people around us, all mixed into the flavours, stirred deep into every dish. How each person likes something a certain way: less spice, more yogurt, their favourite fresh herbs. It's the same wherever you go around the world: secret family recipes passed down, recreating how your mother used to cook your childhood meals, the traditions and rituals you want to pass to your own children. It's where we originate from; it's our past and it's also the future.

When you sleep on the ground, when you are frightened for your life, when you go through tough times, you have a different relationship with your family. It makes you appreciate all your loved ones so much more. But I hope you don't have to go through what I have to love your family as much as I do. Just start loving them now.

KHUBZ

Flatbread

I demoed this on the BBC's *Saturday Kitchen*, so you can have a look on the website if you need visual help on how to make them. I always like to make extra so I can use them for recipes like fattoush on page 107.

TO MAKE

❖ ❖ ❖ ❖ ❖ ❖ ❖ ❖ ❖ ❖ ❖ ❖ ❖ ❖ ❖ ❖ ❖

570g white bread flour,
  plus extra for dusting
1 teaspoon salt
1 teaspoon sugar
1 tablespoon fast-action
  dried yeast
400ml lukewarm water

Mix together the flour, salt, sugar and yeast in the bowl of an electric stand mixer, or a large bowl.

Gradually pour in the water and mix again, or tip out onto a floured surface and knead to a soft, non-sticky dough (4–6 minutes in a stand mixer or 8 minutes by hand). Cover and leave to rest for 30–60 minutes until doubled in size (the time will differ depending on how warm your house is).

Knock the rested dough back into the bowl then tip onto a floured surface and divide into 12–14 balls, each about the size of a golf ball. Cover with a tea towel and rest again for another 30 minutes.

Using a rolling pin, roll the balls out into circles, about 5mm thick.

Heat a wok upside down over a medium-high heat and spray with water. Place one of the pieces of dough on the upturned wok and cook for 30 seconds, then flip and cook on the other side for 20 seconds more. You can just do this in a frying pan if you prefer. Remove and wrap in a damp tea towel while you repeat with the remaining dough, spraying the wok with water between each one.

LABNEH

This makes a lot of labneh but it can last up to 10 days in the fridge. I've given the original, basic recipe below but if you want some extra flavour, you can add any herbs you want, either as you make it or later on before serving. We mix 2 tablespoons dried mint and 1 tablespoon dried thyme into the yogurt to make the labneh we have on the menu at the restaurant. In Syria we don't add a squeeze of lemon, but I wanted to do this in this recipe because the yogurt here is slightly sweeter.

You can treat this just as you would any soft cheese – spread it on toast or pitta, eat it in the morning with za'atar, olives and a drizzle of olive oil. A favourite addition is okra deep-fried in coriander oil (page 37), topped with fresh coriander and Aleppo or red chilli flakes.

TO MAKE

✧ ✧ ✧ ✧ ✧ ✧ ✧ ✧ ✧ ✧ ✧ ✧ ✧ ✧ ✧ ✧

1kg Greek-style yogurt
Small squeeze of lemon juice
 (¼ lemon)
1 teaspoon salt

Mix the yogurt, lemon juice and salt together very well, then put in a strainer to drain – we have dedicated strainers for this, but you can put the yogurt in a clean, dry tea towel in a colander set over a bowl. Place in the fridge to drain for 12 hours, then transfer the drained yogurt to an airtight container and keep in the fridge.

TOO MUCH?

✧ ✧ ✧ ✧ ✧ ✧ ✧ ✧ ✧ ✧ ✧ ✧ ✧ ✧ ✧ ✧

If you really think you have too much, there are lots of ways to use it up. One of the best ways is to turn it into *labneh mudaebila*.

Line a tray with a clean, dry tea towel or J-cloth and spread the labneh from the recipe above on top. Keep it in the fridge for 2 days to dry it out further. Roll the dried labneh into balls. If you like you can now roll it in sumac, za'atar, dried mint or any other flavouring. Store in a sterilised jar, covered in olive oil, and it will keep for several months.

MTAFAYT BAMYEH

SERVES 2

Okra and labneh

TO MAKE

✦ ✦ ✦ ✦ ✦ ✦ ✦ ✦ ✦ ✦ ✦ ✦ ✦ ✦ ✦ ✦ ✦ ✦

250g okra
2 tablespoons olive oil
4 tablespoons coriander oil
 (page 37)
Small pinch of sumac
Small pinch of Aleppo
 chilli flakes
200g labneh (see page 87
 for homemade)

Wash the okra, trim the stalks off the ends and dry in a clean tea towel. Then thinly slice into long strips.

Heat the olive oil and, once the oil is hot, add the okra and fry on all sides for about 5 minutes until golden but still crunchy.

Remove from the pan and add to a large bowl. Add the coriander oil, sumac and chilli flakes and toss to coat.

Dollop the labneh onto a serving plate, then top with the okra. Finish by pouring over the remaining coriander oil from the bowl.

Serve immediately.

BABA GANOUSH

Small aubergines are no good here; you need large ones. It's up to you how you char them – at the restaurant we do it over a flame, but you can also do it in the oven; I've given both methods below. You can top the baba ganoush with anything from the toppings list below, or just have it on its own.

Pictured overleaf.

TO MAKE

✦ ✦ ✦ ✦ ✦ ✦ ✦ ✦ ✦ ✦ ✦ ✦ ✦ ✦ ✦ ✦ ✦

3 large aubergines
Juice of 1 lemon
4 confit garlic cloves (page 53)
1 teaspoon ground cumin
1 teaspoon salt
100g tahini
Olive oil, to drizzle (optional,
　see below)

Starting at the stalk, use a sharp knife to score lengthways from top to bottom all the way around on both sides of each aubergine. Don't go too far into the aubergine – about 5mm. This will make it easier when you come to scoop out the soft, cooked flesh.

If you're charring the aubergines in the oven, preheat the oven to 240°C/Fan 220°C/gas 9, then place in the oven on a baking tray for 30 minutes, turning them over as they cook. If you're charring them over a flame (either on your hob or on a flame grill/barbecue), hold them carefully with tongs and keep turning them over. You're looking for the skins to be really blackened and charred, and the aubergine to almost collapse. Each aubergine has its own shape and size, and water content, but you can check inside the score line; when it is dark brown just inside, that means the middle is done. Remove from the heat and leave to cool a little.

When you can hold it with your fingers, split each aubergine in half and, keeping one half back of each still in its skin, scoop out the flesh of the other halves into a food processor (discarding the skins on these halves). Add the reserved aubergine halves – including the skin – to the food processor with the lemon juice, garlic, cumin and salt, and process until semi-smooth. The charred skin adds a really intense smoky flavor. Mix through the tahini, then serve with a stack of flatbreads, drizzled with olive oil or with one of the topping suggestions opposite.

Alternatively, you can finely chop the ingredients instead of processing, for a chunkier result.

TOPPINGS

- Tahini sauce (page 54), drizzled over the top
- Pomegranate molasses, pomegranate seeds and a drizzle of olive oil
- Chopped cherry tomatoes and olive oil
- Chopped rosemary
- Chopped parsley (we usually add this on top of any extra topping we use)

My very favourite topping — Shred 2 – 3 spring onions into 5mm strips. Fry with 2 crushed garlic cloves in 50ml extra virgin olive oil. Add a pinch of salt. We often like to add a little chopped rosemary on top as well.

MUHAMMARA

It's important to use romano (long) peppers here as the skins aren't as tough as on bell peppers. If you can't get hold of them, use bell peppers, but after roasting, add them to a bowl, immediately cover with clingfilm and allow to cool. You'll then be able to easily peel off the tough charred skins.

TO MAKE

❖ ❖ ❖ ❖ ❖ ❖ ❖ ❖ ❖ ❖ ❖ ❖ ❖ ❖ ❖ ❖ ❖ ❖

5 red romano peppers
2 red chillies
75g walnuts
4 tablespoons red pepper paste
1 teaspoon ground coriander
1 teaspoon ground cumin
½ teaspoon salt

Preheat the oven to 220°C/Fan 200°C/gas 7. Place the peppers and chillies on a large baking tray in a single layer and roast for 20 – 25 minutes, turning halfway through, until the skin is blackened and charred on both sides. Allow to cool slightly then pull off the stems from each pepper and chilli.

Spread the walnuts out on another baking tray and toast in the oven for 5 minutes. Remove and allow to cool.

Add the chillies, red pepper paste and spices to a food processor and blitz to a paste. Now add the roasted peppers, walnuts and salt and pulse carefully until you have a rough, chunky consistency. You don't want a smooth paste here.

TO SERVE

❖ ❖ ❖ ❖ ❖ ❖ ❖ ❖ ❖ ❖ ❖ ❖ ❖ ❖ ❖ ❖ ❖ ❖

2 tablespoons pomegranate
  molasses
Small bunch of parsley,
  finely chopped
½ red onion, finely chopped
Handful of pomegranate seeds
Extra virgin olive oil, to drizzle

Spoon into a bowl or onto a plate and drizzle over the pomegranate molasses. Garnish with parsley, red onion, pomegranate seeds and a drizzle of olive oil.

LABAN

Yogurt

MAKES 2 LITRES

2 litres best-quality whole milk
4 tablespoons 10-day-old homemade yogurt

Bring the milk to the boil in a large pot. Take off
the heat then transfer to a ceramic/clay heatproof
container/pot that ideally isn't clear. Let it cool
until you can put your finger in it comfortably with
it still being hot (roughly 45–50°C if you have
a thermometer).

Add the yogurt and mix until combined. Cover with
a tea towel or large cloth then wrap it all up in a blanket
or large piece of thick fabric and place in a cool, dry
place out of the sun for at least 12 hours.

Remove the blanket/fabric and tea towel/cloth and
put in the fridge, uncovered, for another 12 hours.

Keep it in the fridge and use the last few tablespoons
to repeat the process, or make labneh or labneh
mudaebila (see page 87).

LABAN BIKHIAR

Yogurt salad

Yogurt should be naturally sour but
some brands you get in the UK taste
sweet. So get the best-quality sour
yogurt if you can find it.

MAKES 400G

½ cucumber
350g Greek-style yogurt or homemade yogurt
  (see left)
2 garlic cloves, finely grated or smashed to a paste
2 tablespoons dried mint
Good pinch of flaky sea salt
Juice of ½ lemon (optional)

Grate the cucumber into a mixing bowl and add the
yogurt, garlic, dried mint and salt, and mix together.
If your yogurt is sweet, add the lemon juice to taste.

MY MOTHER

MY MOTHER WAS LIKE my Damascus: generous, hardworking and overflowing with love for everyone around her. And also like my Damascus, she died without me being able to properly say goodbye, without being able to get that closure. But that doesn't mean I don't love them both still. I dream of them both, I speak of them both, but I know I will never see either of them in my life again.

I owe everything to my mother. Every single thing I do or think or say has been influenced by her. My cooking, my recipes, my lips, my short fingers! That I am able to speak English. Even the décor at the restaurant is inspired by the things she loved: the plants and pots and collections she kept in her home. I see something of my mother in each of my daughters, and it makes me love them even more.

I don't talk about my father much because I look so much like him. He used to tell me that he wanted me to be a better version of him. I think in life the only people you can genuinely say you want to do better than you, with true happiness, are your own children! As the eldest son, when I was six or seven years old, my father would take me to show me around the family business, to see what I would inherit one day, what I would become. This was my path. Almost my entire family was in textiles – uncles, aunts, cousins. It was what we did. The natural career for me was fashion designing – and I loved it! I did it for a long time, before I found my way into food. In Syria, you have to do military service when you are 18, but even as a kid I was never interested in playing with guns. So, instead, I went to Dubai to study fashion and even set up my own design studio. Here I was, 20 or 21 with a successful fashion business. But in my heart I knew it wasn't for me.

I set up my first restaurant in 2000 and it was a huge moment for my mother. She was the one who had taught me to cook, who had taught me everything I knew about food. The rest of the family were working in fashion or designing, but I had chosen restaurants and cooking. Somehow, my mother felt like she had won, and she was very, very proud.

My mother was the most brilliant person, full of joy. I wanted her to see the world more, to experience life more, but her happiness came from being creative, from being productive. She wove rugs, drew on glass and painted on silk. I designed a dark blue jacket and she embroidered gold thread on top, and it was the most beautiful thing I'd ever seen. She was so creative, always searching for something new.

She had the most beautiful smile, she was truly radiant because she was comfortable in herself. She had an inner peace. She knew how to encourage others to be the best they could be, and she would always find a way to help. If someone was struggling, she'd be there for them. She tutored English and maths, and loved to work with the totally lost causes, those who everyone thought had no hope! She had her own special way of explaining things and you could listen to her for hours. She not only taught me cooking, she taught me how to be a better person. She taught me more things than I can ever understand, than I will every fully appreciate – not to be selfish, but to help others, to be kind. I have a wonderful relationship with my wife and my daughters, I think mostly because of her. She used to take care of everyone around her, her family, her neighbours. Everyone loved her. When I left Syria, I couldn't bear leaving my wife and children behind, but she eased my anxiety, knowing she'd look after them too.

Although she lived a relatively short life, it was a full life. If she was alive now, I honestly think my life would be so much easier. I could just ask her, rather than wondering 'what would mama do?' I know it's futile, but a big part of me thinks about how I would love her to see me now, to talk to her about what I'm doing. I think she would have loved it, seeing people coming together to enjoy Syrian food, my recipes, her recipes living on.

My mother passed away when I had been in the UK just fifty days. I was alone and she was unwell in the hospital. Two days before she died, I asked my aunt to let me speak with her because I had this feeling it might be the last time. But my aunt told me to stop talking in that way, that she would be fine, not to start worrying everyone. My wife, Batool, was with her just before she passed, and says my mother opened her eyes and said to her: 'Tell Imad I love him, and that I am pleased with him. He has my approval.'

TABBOULEH

The key to this lies with the lemon, black pepper and parsley. It's supposed to be sour and fresh to break the richness of a main dish; we would never order this on its own.

TO MAKE

✧ ✧ ✧ ✧ ✧ ✧ ✧ ✧ ✧ ✧ ✧ ✧ ✧ ✧ ✧ ✧ ✧ ✧ ✧ ✧

100g fine bulgur wheat
2 lemons
Good pinch of salt
1 teaspoon ground black pepper
2 – 3 big bunches of parsley, very finely chopped
1 little gem lettuce, very finely chopped, plus leaves to serve
3 tomatoes, deseeded and finely diced
1 small red onion, finely diced

In a bowl, wash the bulgur in cold water, then drain and place back in the bowl with enough fresh water to just cover it. Squeeze in the juice from 1½ of the lemons and set aside to soak for 1 hour. If after soaking there is excess liquid, drain before using.

Add the salt and black pepper and mix with a fork to separate the grains. Very finely chop the remaining half lemon and add to the bulgur along with the parsley, lettuce, tomatoes and red onion. Mix everything together well.

TO SERVE

✧ ✧ ✧ ✧ ✧ ✧ ✧ ✧ ✧ ✧ ✧ ✧ ✧ ✧ ✧ ✧ ✧ ✧ ✧ ✧

Handful of pomegranate seeds
Lemon slices
Extra virgin olive oil

Arrange a few lettuce leaves in a bowl and spoon in the tabbouleh. Serve topped with pomegranate seeds, some lemon slices and a drizzle of olive oil.

JIRJIR

Rocket salad

TO MAKE

✧ ✧ ✧ ✧ ✧ ✧ ✧ ✧ ✧ ✧ ✧ ✧ ✧ ✧ ✧ ✧ ✧ ✧ ✧

Grated zest and juice of 1 lemon

3 tablespoons extra virgin
  olive oil

1 tablespoon za'atar

1 teaspoon sumac

250g halloumi,
  cut into 2cm cubes

3 handfuls of rocket leaves

400g watermelon,
  cut into 2cm cubes

Add the lemon zest and juice, oil, za'atar and sumac to a bowl and mix well. Add the halloumi and toss well to combine.

Add the rocket and watermelon to a large platter, followed by the dressed halloumi. You can toss everything together or just serve as is.

SALAD VARIATIONS

BIWAS

This is a very flavoursome salad, which is very refreshing to the tastebuds.

SERVES 4 AS A SIDE

1 large red onion, thinly sliced
Large handful of parsley, finely chopped
3 tablespoons pomegranate molasses
Juice of ½ lemon
Pinch of salt
Pinch of sumac

Mix all the ingredients together in a bowl.

DAKA

A famous dish in Palestine, this very traditional Syrian salad can be served with fish. It is refreshing and zesty.

SERVES 4 AS A SIDE

2 garlic cloves
Pinch of salt
1 green chilli, sliced
2 ripe vine tomatoes, diced
4 spring onions, chopped
Handful of parsley, roughly chopped
1 tablespoon extra virgin olive oil
Juice of 1 lemon

Very finely chop the garlic with the pinch of salt. Alternatively, mash them together using a pestle and mortar.

Add to a bowl with the chilli, tomatoes, spring onions and parsley, then mix through the olive oil and lemon juice and serve.

CHERMOULA

This is full of fresh herbs, but thanks to the oil this will keep well in the fridge in an airtight container.

SERVES 4 AS A SIDE

Small handful of coriander
Small handful of parsley
2 garlic cloves
1 preserved lemon
1 tablespoon capers
100ml extra virgin olive oil
¼ teaspoon ground coriander
¼ teaspoon ground cumin
Grated zest and juice of ½ lemon
Salt

Finely chop the coriander and parsley leaves and stalks, garlic, preserved lemon and capers together, and add them to a bowl with the oil, ground coriander, cumin, lemon zest and juice and a pinch of salt, or to taste. Mix to combine. Alternatively, add everything to a blender and pulse until semi-smooth.

This will keep, covered, in the fridge, for up to a week.

FATTOUSH SALAD

TO MAKE THE FATTOUSH

❖ ❖ ❖ ❖ ❖ ❖ ❖ ❖ ❖ ❖ ❖ ❖ ❖ ❖ ❖ ❖

½ teaspoon sumac
½ teaspoon dried thyme
½ teaspoon dried oregano
Small pinch of salt
1 tablespoon olive oil
1 thin flatbread (see page 82 for
   homemade) or flour tortilla,
   cut into thin strips
Orange-infused oil (optional;
   page 37), to serve

Preheat the oven to 200°C/Fan 180°C/gas 6.

Mix together the sumac, dried thyme and oregano, salt and olive oil and toss the flatbread strips through to coat. Place on a baking tray in a single layer and toast in the oven for 5 minutes until crisp and golden.

FOR THE DRESSING

❖ ❖ ❖ ❖ ❖ ❖ ❖ ❖ ❖ ❖ ❖ ❖ ❖ ❖ ❖

2 tablespoons extra virgin olive oil
1 tablespoon apple cider vinegar
½ tablespoon pomegranate
   molasses
1 teaspoon sumac

Add all the dressing ingredients to a jar and shake to combine.

FOR THE SMASHED AVOCADO

❖ ❖ ❖ ❖ ❖ ❖ ❖ ❖ ❖ ❖ ❖ ❖ ❖ ❖ ❖

1 avocado, peeled and pitted
½ red onion, very finely diced
Juice of ½ lemon
½ red chilli, finely diced (optional)

Mix all the smashed avocado ingredients together in a bowl, mash with a fork until smooth, then set aside.

FOR THE SALAD

❖ ❖ ❖ ❖ ❖ ❖ ❖ ❖ ❖ ❖ ❖ ❖ ❖ ❖ ❖

1 Cos lettuce, finely sliced
100g vine or beef tomatoes, cut
   into 1cm dice
100g pomegranate seeds
3 baby cucumbers, cut into 1cm dice
40g green olives, pitted and torn

Toss the salad ingredients together with the dressing. Top with the smashed avocado, followed by the toasted flatbread, then finish with the orange oil, if using.

SAROJA

Baby aubergines and cheese

Saroja is a neighbourhood in Damascus close to where I lived, and this dish always reminds me of there.

FOR THE VEGETABLES

✣ ✣ ✣ ✣ ✣ ✣ ✣ ✣ ✣ ✣ ✣ ✣ ✣ ✣ ✣ ✣ ✣ ✣ ✣

350g baby aubergines
90g panko breadcrumbs
2 eggs
1 tablespoon za'atar
1 teaspoon salt
½ teaspoon ground cumin
A few grinds of cracked
 black pepper
Small handful of parsley,
 finely chopped
Olive oil, for drizzling

Preheat the oven to 200°C/Fan 180°C/gas 6.

Remove the stems from the aubergines and slice each in half lengthways, then slice each half across into half-moons 1cm thick. Add the slices to a bowl of salty water while you get on with the breadcrumb mix.

Get 2 medium bowls and add the breadcrumbs to one and the eggs to the other. Beat the eggs well with the za'atar, salt, cumin, black pepper and parsley.

Drain the aubergines and pat dry with kitchen towel.

Line a large, low-sided baking tray with baking paper then dip each aubergine slice into the egg mixture, followed by the breadcrumbs, making sure they are all evenly coated. Place the breaded aubergine slices on the lined baking tray.

Drizzle each slice with a little olive oil then bake in the oven for 20 minutes.

FOR THE CHEESE

✣ ✣ ✣ ✣ ✣ ✣ ✣ ✣ ✣ ✣ ✣ ✣ ✣ ✣ ✣ ✣ ✣ ✣ ✣

100g feta, crumbled
100g halloumi, grated
1 teaspoon black sesame seeds
1 teaspoon toasted white
 sesame seeds
4 tablespoons date molasses
2 tablespoons sour cherry molasses
Small handful of mint leaves,
 chopped

Put the feta, halloumi and all the sesame seeds in a bowl and mix to combine.

In a separate small bowl, stir together the date and sour cherry molasses.

To serve, add the cheese mixture to a platter or plates and top with the crispy aubergine. Drizzle over the molasses dressing and finish with chopped mint.

SBANAKH KHUDRA

Green spinach

TO MAKE

✦ ✦

800g large-leaf spinach
50ml extra virgin olive oil
1 red onion, finely chopped
1 teaspoon ground black pepper
3 garlic cloves, smashed to a pulp
Handful of coriander,
   roughly chopped
2 tablespoons pomegranate
   molasses
Handful of pomegranate seeds
Good pinch of flaky sea salt
Plain rice, to serve

Start by thoroughly washing the spinach in a large colander,
in batches if you need to. Remove any large, tough central stems,
then roughly tear and set aside.

Add the oil to a large saucepan over a medium-high heat, then add
the red onion and black pepper and cook for 3–4 minutes until just
softened. Now add the garlic and coriander and cook for a minute
before adding the spinach. Depending on what type of spinach you
have, it will take 1–3 minutes to wilt, so keep stirring it until just
cooked and still bright green.

Transfer to a serving plate and top with the pomegranate molasses,
pomegranate seeds and flaky sea salt. Serve alongside plain rice.

MTUMA

Crushed new potatoes

TO MAKE

✧ ✧ ✧ ✧ ✧ ✧ ✧ ✧ ✧ ✧ ✧ ✧ ✧ ✧ ✧ ✧ ✧ ✧ ✧

1kg new potatoes
4 tablespoons extra virgin
  olive oil
2 garlic cloves, crushed
50g salted butter
Small bunch of parsley,
  finely chopped
4 spring onions, very finely sliced
1 teaspoon sumac
Salt and ground black pepper

Preheat the oven to 200°C/Fan 180°C/gas 6.

Boil the potatoes in a large pot of salted water for 8 – 10 minutes until soft. Drain, then allow to steam for a few minutes.

Add the potatoes to a large, low-sided baking tray with 3 tablespoons of the olive oil and a good pinch each of salt and pepper. Crush each potato lightly by pressing down on them with the bottom of a glass, so they just break open. Roast in the oven for 20 minutes.

Mix the crushed garlic and butter to a paste, then remove the potatoes from the oven and add the garlic butter. Toss to coat all the potatoes then return to the oven for a further 5 minutes until crispy and golden.

FOR THE CHERMOULA YOGURT

✧ ✧ ✧ ✧ ✧ ✧ ✧ ✧ ✧ ✧ ✧ ✧ ✧ ✧ ✧ ✧ ✧

150g thick Greek-style yogurt
75g chermoula (page 105)
50g tahini

Meanwhile, mix together the ingredients for the chermoula yogurt and set aside.

Dollop the chermoula yogurt onto a large platter, then pile the crispy, buttery potatoes on top. Sprinkle over the parsley, spring onions, sumac and a little more salt and pepper to taste, then serve immediately.

FALAFEL

People ask how many falafel you should make, but in my opinion there is no such thing as too many falafel! If it's too much for you, your neighbour can have some – in Damascus, if our neighbours can smell what we're cooking, we have to take round a small plate of it for them to taste.

Falafel are not made with cooked chickpeas, but with dried chickpeas soaked in water, so you absolutely cannot use chickpeas from a tin or jar. I use a traditional meat mincer to make falafel, which is a good investment if you're going to make them a lot. Otherwise, you can use a food processor, although it will make a wetter mixture. The nice thing about Damascan falafel is it doesn't include any fresh herbs, which means there's no chance of them going soggy as they cook.

You can serve falafel on a plate, as part of a mezze. Or use them in a wrap or pitta, as on page 122.

Sumac and tahini are a must for serving.

TO MAKE

❖ ❖ ❖ ❖ ❖ ❖ ❖ ❖ ❖ ❖ ❖ ❖ ❖ ❖ ❖ ❖ ❖

500g dried chickpeas,
  soaked for at least 14 hours
  (see instructions on page 68)
4 garlic cloves
½ onion, roughly chopped
  or quartered
1 teaspoon garlic powder
2 tablespoons ground coriander
1 tablespoon ground cumin
½ teaspoon bicarbonate of soda
1 tablespoon salt
50g sesame seeds
100 – 150ml room-temperature
  water
Rapeseed oil, for deep-frying

Put the soaked, drained chickpeas with the garlic and onion through a meat mincer into a bowl (or process in a food processor if you don't have a meat mincer). Then stir in the spices, bicarbonate of soda and salt. If you are using a food processor, pulse it gently; it should have a fine-ish sandy consistency. You can use the falafel mixture straight away or keep it in the fridge at this stage for up to 2 days.

Mix through the sesame seeds and enough water to be able to gather a ball of mixture and for it to loosely stay together. It shouldn't be too wet – just enough to form a loose patty.

Pour a 10cm depth of oil into a deep, heavy-based pan and heat to 180°C. To test if the oil is hot enough, drop in a little piece of falafel; if it bubbles and rises to the top, you are ready to go.

I use a special falafel tool for shaping, which you can pick up fairly inexpensively online. My falafel have a hole in the middle, resulting in a crisper texture. Otherwise, use 2 dessertspoons to shape the mixture, or you can just roll into balls and flatten them down with your hands. Your falafel should be about 4cm across.

Carefully lower the shaped falafels into the hot oil, in batches so you don't overcrowd the pan (or the temperature of the oil will drop and you won't have nice crispy falafel).

Let them crisp up for 2 minutes until golden brown, then move the oil around a little to cook them evenly all over. They should be fully cooked, golden brown and crisp in 4 minutes. Scoop out with a slotted spoon onto kitchen paper to absorb excess oil.

FALAFEL WRAP

Put each of the wrap ingredients in a bowl on the table so people can make their own, adding as much or as little as they like.

TO MAKE

❖ ❖ ❖ ❖ ❖ ❖ ❖ ❖ ❖ ❖ ❖ ❖ ❖ ❖ ❖ ❖ ❖ ❖

Breads – pitta bread or flatbreads
  (see page 82 for homemade)
Hummus (page 68)
5 or 6 falafels per person
Sliced pickled cucumbers
  (optional, page 56)
Sliced tomato halves
Lemon slices
Chopped parsley
Pickled chillies/Aleppo chilli flakes
Tahini sauce (page 54)
Sumac

Spread each bread with a generous spoonful of hummus. Smash the falafel on top of the hummus, pressing it down into the hummus. Top with pickled cucumber slices, diced tomato, lemon slices, chopped parsley, pickled chillies or chilli flakes, a drizzle of tahini sauce and a pinch of sumac.

THE MOMENT I ARRIVED in London, I felt free. In every other city I had been in, the ten countries I'd travelled across, people would look at me and I would assume they would think, 'Oh, another Syrian refugee coming through.' In London, I was invisible. I looked like everyone else. There are people from all nationalities, all doing their own thing. No one even noticed me. I was in awe. I fell in love with this city immediately.

My journey from Syria to the UK is one that thousands of Syrians have taken. It's not a choice we make, we don't choose to be refugees. It's not like we decided one day to leave behind a comfortable life to live in Europe. And the journey is every bit as difficult, as exhausting, as dehumanising, as frightening as you imagine it is from the stories you've already heard.

My story, like so many others, began with me leaving my family behind in Damascus. I knew it was unsafe for them there; in another life before all this, I couldn't have imagined leaving them in this way, but it was our only option. I fear for the future of Syria and can't even bring myself to imagine our life if we were all still there today. Getting to safety, and then getting them to join me, was the only way out.

From Damascus, I travelled by car into Lebanon and then on up through Turkey. In Turkey I was put in touch with a smuggler who I paid so I could get on a boat to Greece. It was a small, rubber dingy designed to hold nine people. There were fifty-six of us crammed in, including a pregnant woman and 12 children. I have no idea how it didn't sink, how we all survived. Thinking about it now, about the risks we were all taking, still haunts me. But arriving in Greece – in Europe! – was the most incredible feeling. It was 2 August 2015. I won't ever forget. By this stage in all of our journeys, though, having come so far already, having left so much behind, with so much uncertainty still ahead, we were broken people. Whoever we used to be when we lived in Syria was gone, we were brought down to nothing, we had been made to feel like we were nothing. But, for a little while in Greece we had our humanity restored. We were met by volunteers who welcomed us, who showed us the way to go next, who made us feel safe. The Greek coast guards had rescue boats that they'd launch into the sea, but instead of helping those refugees who were making that terrifying journey across the water, they'd damage their boats, they'd prevent them landing on the shores. I have learnt so many lessons about myself, about human beings, about the world since the war started, but the most powerful realisation I have come to is that there are two types of people. Yes, there are those who willingly sabotage the boats of desperate people fleeing for their lives. But there are also those who will welcome you with open arms, with love, with handwritten signs that read 'You are safe'. I had left Syria with my faith in everything completely destroyed, but my journey, however dangerous at times, has helped me believe in the goodness in people again.

From Greece, I walked hundreds of miles to Macedonia, and then caught a train into Serbia. I cycled all the way through Serbia, and another smuggler helped me into Hungary. The boat crossing to Greece was traumatising, but I think the most difficult part of the journey for me was in Hungary. Six men, including me, hiding in the back of an old Peugeot with the back seats taken out. Can you imagine trying to fit us all in? And then out of nowhere a seventh man jumped in to join us. We had no choice but to let him come with us, as he'd have shouted and given us away if we'd said no. We were crammed in, squashed up against each other for four hours as our driver, who was drunk, drove us to Vienna. When we arrived, he shouted for us to get out, but all of our arms and legs were totally numb and none of us could move.

From Vienna, another train took me to Stuttgart, in Germany, and for many refugees, this is where their journey ends. Germany has helped so many people find refuge, to begin new lives, and I could have stayed there too. But I had family in England, I spoke English already. I am too old to learn a new language and I need to speak it well so I can work. So I carried on from Germany to Paris. I spent a couple of nights in Paris, while I rested and figured out what to do next. That was when I started to hear the word Calais. I'd heard of Calais before, in passing, in my former life as a textiler back in Syria and in Dubai. There is a beautiful, silk-like fabric called Dantelle de Calais – Made in Calais – that is used for making wedding dresses. It felt like a sign: I was going to Calais.

When I arrived in Calais, it was not as I'd imagined. It was terrifying. The Jungle – the camp where refugees like me were staying – was too dangerous, too crowded. In the area around it, the air was charged with a strange energy, like something bad could happen at any minute. Instead, I slept on the steps of a church for 64 days with several other Syrian refugees. I'd left Syria nine days before, and then here I was for two months, with many, many failed attempts to cross into the UK. The church was empty, mostly unused except for funerals, when we would remove our belongings and clean the entrance way. You'd think I would have been at my lowest at this point and yet here was where my hope returned. I found cooking again, with one knife (no more, in case people thought I was a threat) and a small hot plate donated to us. We'd get leftovers from the supermarket, from the Carrefour, and with those leftovers, with whatever we had, I'd cook the dishes I loved from home, adapted, of course, depending on what we had, and people found joy where they could in eating what I made. I think it restored in all of us the faith that things could, and would, get better.

The closest I came to successfully making it across to the UK was on a trip back to Paris. I'd been put in touch with a smuggler there, who connected me with another Syrian, Hassan Akkad. I didn't know him, but we'd been neighbours in Damascus and we knew each other's friends. He had been filming parts of his journey on his phone and his story was later used in the BAFTA-winning documentary series, *Exodus: Our Journey to Europe*. He's a great friend of mine now, but back then I just thought he was one of the smugglers, and neither of us quite trusted each other. Hassan delivered a fake ID to me, and brought it to where I was staying in Paris. When he arrived at the hotel, I was wearing the same shirt as in the photo and he told me to change as it'd be too obvious it wasn't genuine! The plan was for us to fly from Charles de Gaulle airport into Heathrow. Hassan would go after me and if I was successful he'd follow on the next flight. If I didn't make it, I'd go back to Paris and I'd get my money back. It was all incredibly organised – honestly, the smuggler network is more efficient than the UK Home Office!

Hours later, I was standing at the airport gate waiting to board an EasyJet flight to the UK, my fake Greek passport in my hand, my new name Buros. It was all going to be OK. This was it, the moment I'd been dreaming of for months. Then, I heard a voice over the loudspeakers calling for Buros. I froze. I was told I had to go to the ticket office as there was a problem with my ticket.

Entering the ticket office, I had no idea what was about to happen. But I knew it couldn't be good. The woman behind the desk asked me where my passport had come from and I told her it was mine. She then handed me a piece of paper with some Greek written on it. I looked down at it and my heart sank. She said, 'if you can read this, I'll let you go'. It was all over. I told her I couldn't read it, but that I was just doing my best. I was just trying to do what I could for my family. To be safe. She looked right at me and told me that the police would be in her office in five minutes.I sank down, defeated. But then, she said 'no, no, you don't understand. You have five minutes before the police get here – go!'. I couldn't believe what I was hearing. I had five minutes to escape. She told me to get on the train, not to wait for the bus, and to head back to Paris. I made it outside into the fresh air and still couldn't take in what had just happened. I didn't have enough money for the train, so I stood at the bus stop waiting. Then I saw the woman again, she'd followed me out and asked me why I was still there. When I explained, she gave me her own metro ticket and also her phone number. Before she left she took my arm and told me that my ID was great, it was a really great passport, but whoever had arranged my flight had already booked fifty people one-way on the same credit card and that's why it had been flagged. She said goodbye and, as so often on this crazy journey, I felt as though I'd been saved by an angel.

Hassan was in jail. He'd never made it across to the UK. He didn't even board his flight. The police left him in a bare cell overnight and then drove him up the motorway and left him on the side of the road in the pouring rain. We didn't have each other's phone numbers, but he came to the hotel where he'd delivered my passport, to the hotel I was staying in, hoping I'd be there. My room phone rang, and reception said I had a visitor downstairs. I didn't know what to expect because I didn't know anyone! When Hassan saw me, he started crying. He was cold, wet, miserable and completely lost. They'd told him I was in the UK, and so seeing each other was an incredibly emotional moment for us both. We were reunited, afraid, still stuck in Paris, but alive and free. We had to make a new plan. In the morning we headed back to Calais.

DUKKAH SALAD

Heritage tomato, roast fennel and dukkah

SERVES 2 AS A MAIN
OR 4 AS A SIDE

Make this in summer when the tomatoes are at their best. The better the tomato, the better this will taste, so splash out and get the good ones.

TO MAKE

❖ ❖ ❖ ❖ ❖ ❖ ❖ ❖ ❖ ❖ ❖ ❖ ❖ ❖ ❖ ❖ ❖ ❖

1 fennel bulb
2 tablespoons olive oil
1 teaspoon za'atar
300g assorted heritage tomatoes, cut into chunks
2 tablespoons good-quality extra virgin olive oil
Grated zest and juice of ½ lemon
2 tablespoons dukkah (page 29)
150g soft goat's cheese
Small handful of fresh tarragon leaves
Salt

Preheat the oven to 200°C/Fan 180°C/gas 6.

Cut the fennel bulb into 6–8 wedges, depending on how large your fennel is. Toss in the olive oil, za'atar and salt to taste, place on an oven tray and roast for 25–30 minutes until soft, slightly crisp and golden. Set aside to cool slightly.

Toss the tomatoes in a little salt and the extra virgin olive oil, lemon zest and juice and dukkah. Roughly crumble the cheese and place on a large serving plate, followed by the roasted fennel and then the tomatoes. Finish with the tarragon leaves.

HARAA ASBAEU

Sometimes when I can't find the right pasta for this, I buy pappardelle or fettuccine and either chop it up if it's fresh, or scrunch up dried to make small pieces.

FOR THE TAMARIND SAUCE

❖ ❖ ❖ ❖ ❖ ❖ ❖ ❖ ❖ ❖ ❖ ❖ ❖ ❖ ❖

35g tamarind block
200ml water

To make the tamarind sauce, crumble the dried tamarind block into a saucepan and add the water. Bring to the boil over a medium heat and boil for at least 30 minutes to extract all the flavour and reduce the water. Strain through a sieve into a bowl; use a spoon to squash it through and scrape underneath into the bowl. You'll be left with a little under 100ml and will have a really intense flavour. If you end up with a bit less than this, that's fine – it's all about the flavour.

TO MAKE

❖ ❖ ❖ ❖ ❖ ❖ ❖ ❖ ❖ ❖ ❖ ❖ ❖ ❖ ❖

2 flatbreads (see page 82 for
   homemade) or flour tortillas
1 tablespoon olive oil
1 teaspoon sumac
250g dried brown lentils
1.5 litres just-boiled water
200g small square pasta
   (or any small pasta,
   or see introduction)
5 tablespoons coriander oil
   (page 37)
2 tablespoons pomegranate
   molasses
1 teaspoon ground cumin
1 quantity crispy onions (page 54)
Handful of pomegranate seeds
Salt

Preheat the oven to 200°C/Fan 180°C/gas 6.

Cut the flatbreads into 1cm strips and toss with the olive oil, sumac and a pinch of salt. Spread out on an oven tray and place in the oven for 3–5 minutes until crisp and toasted.

Wash the lentils, then place in a saucepan with the just-boiled water. Add salt and boil for 20 minutes until just cooked. Now stir in the pasta and boil for 5–8 minutes, depending on the type and size, until cooked. You should still have a tiny bit of water left in the pot; if not, add a little more boiling water as you want a silky, wet mixture. Take off the heat.

While the lentils and pasta are still warm, add the coriander oil, making sure you're getting a good amount of the chopped coriander leaves too. Stir in the tamarind sauce, a little more salt to taste if needed, the pomegranate molasses and ground cumin. Tip the lentil and pasta mixture onto a large platter and allow to cool completely.

Traditionally we plate the toppings in stripes, starting with the coriander leaves from the oil, then crispy onions, crispy flatbreads, followed by pomegranate seeds, then repeat.

SAJ

TO MAKE

✣ ✣ ✣ ✣ ✣ ✣ ✣ ✣ ✣ ✣ ✣ ✣ ✣ ✣ ✣ ✣ ✣

1 quantity of flatbread dough
   (page 82)

Make the dough according to the instructions on page 82 and leave
to rise.

When your dough has risen, whisk the egg in a bowl, then stir
in the halloumi, parsley and chilli flakes. Or, if using the za'atar, mix
together the oil and za'atar in a small bowl. Knock back the dough,
divide into 12 equal pieces and roll each into a ball. Set aside to rest
for 15–20 minutes, then roll each ball into a 15cm circle, by only
pushing the rolling pin away from you, turning the dough after
each roll (not back and forth; this is to help get an even flatbread).
At this point I lift the flatbread onto a mukhada – a pillowy surface
to help stretch the dough – but you can skip this if you don't have one.

FOR THE TOPPING

✣ ✣ ✣ ✣ ✣ ✣ ✣ ✣ ✣ ✣ ✣ ✣ ✣ ✣ ✣ ✣ ✣

1 egg
100g halloumi, grated
Small handful of parsley,
   finely chopped
Pinch of chilli flakes
OR
3 tablespoons good-quality olive oil
2 tablespoons za'atar

Place a non-stick frying pan over a medium-high heat and flip
a flatbread into the pan. Cook for 30–40 seconds until lightly
brown, then flip over and spoon over your topping of choice
(the cheese and egg mix or the za'atar oil). Turn down the heat
to medium and continue to cook for 1–2 minutes until the cheese
has melted (if using) and the flatbread is crisp on the bottom.

Serve straight away, while hot.

BATATA HARRA

TO MAKE

❖ ❖ ❖ ❖ ❖ ❖ ❖ ❖ ❖ ❖ ❖ ❖ ❖ ❖ ❖ ❖ ❖ ❖

4 – 5 medium-sized Maris Piper
   or King Edward potatoes,
   peeled and cut into 3cm cubes
4 tablespoons olive oil
5 confit garlic cloves (page 53)
   or 2 peeled raw garlic cloves
½ teaspoon chilli flakes
½ teaspoon ground cumin
½ teaspoon smoked paprika
Large handful of coriander
   leaves, chopped
2 tablespoons extra virgin olive oil
Salt and ground black pepper

Preheat the oven to 220°C/Fan 200°C/gas 7.

Add the potatoes to a large, low-sided roasting tray, toss through the 4 tablespoons of olive oil and a good pinch each of salt and pepper.

Roast in the oven for 30 minutes until crisp and golden all over.

In a small bowl, crush the garlic cloves, then mix in the chilli flakes, cumin, smoked paprika and chopped coriander, along with the extra virgin olive oil. Remove the potatoes from the oven, toss in the spice mix and serve immediately.

FOUR

MAINS

MAINS

+ SHURABAT ENDS 140 +

+ KATIF GHANAM 143 + KEBAB HINDI 144 +

ZAHRAA HARRA 148 + FASULIA BIL ZAYT 150

+ MAHASHI 152 + JAJ BAILFURN 155 +

SYRIAN FISH AND CHIPS WITH TAHINI SAUCE 157

+ MUJADARA 158 + MUJADARA SALAD 160 +

+ KABSA RICE WITH PRAWNS 162 +

+ KABSA RICE WITH CHICKEN 165 +

+ KABSA RICE WITH VEGETABLES 166 +

STUFFED COURGETTES, AUBERGINES AND PEPPERS 167

+ BUTTERED HALIBUT 170 + KUFTAH TAHINI 172 +

KUFTAH BETINJAN 178 + MANZILAT BETINJAN 178

+ TABAKH ROHO 181 + KIPPEH 182 +

KIPPEH MEQLIA 185 + MAKLOUBEH 186

+ MOUSSAKA 192 + FILO RICE 194 +

FWL MUDAMIS 198 + BARGHIL BIALKUSA 198

+ SHISH TAOUK 12 + IMAD'S SAUCE 12 +

SHURABAT ENDS

Lentil soup

TO MAKE

✤ ✤ ✤ ✤ ✤ ✤ ✤ ✤ ✤ ✤ ✤ ✤ ✤ ✤ ✤ ✤ ✤ ✤ ✤ ✤

200g red lentils
50g short-grain rice
50g freekeh
2 tablespoons olive oil
1 tablespoon cumin seeds
2 onions, finely chopped
2 small carrots, peeled and
  roughly chopped
2 garlic cloves, finely chopped
1 teaspoon ground cumin
2 tablespoons safflower
1 teaspoon ground black pepper
½ teaspoon ground coriander
2 tablespoons tomato purée
1.7 litres vegetable or chicken
  stock or water
Salt

Start by washing the lentils, rice and freekeh together in a large sieve until the water runs clear.

In a tall, large pot, heat the olive oil over a medium heat, then add the cumin seeds and toast for a minute. Now add the onions and carrots and cook for 5–8 minutes until soft and a little caramelised. Add the garlic and cook for a further 1–2 minutes until softened.

Add the lentils, rice and freekeh and stir to toast all the grains for 2 minutes before mixing in the ground cumin, 1 tablespoon of the safflower, the black pepper, ground coriander, tomato purée and 2 teaspoons of salt. Once everything is nicely toasted and coated in spices, add the stock or water so it covers everything by at least 6cm.

Bring to the boil, then turn down and simmer for 1 hour until everything is soft.

Process to a thick soup in a blender, adding more water if needed, then add the remaining safflower. Taste and season as necessary.

TO SERVE

✤ ✤ ✤ ✤ ✤ ✤ ✤ ✤ ✤ ✤ ✤ ✤ ✤ ✤ ✤ ✤ ✤ ✤ ✤

Single cream (or mozzarella,
  torn into small pieces)
Small handful of chives,
  finely chopped
4 pitta breads, toasted

Ladle into bowls and top with cream or mozzarella and chives, and serve with toasted pitta bread.

KATIF GHANAM

Lamb shoulder

FOR THE MARINADE

✢ ✢ ✢ ✢ ✢ ✢ ✢ ✢ ✢ ✢ ✢ ✢ ✢ ✢ ✢ ✢ ✢ ✢ ✢

5 garlic cloves, grated
2 tablespoons smoked paprika
1 tablespoon mild Madras
 curry powder
½ tablespoon ground black pepper
3cm piece of fresh ginger, grated
1 tablespoon baharat (page 32)
Juice of 1 lemon
1 tablespoon tomato purée
2 tablespoons red pepper paste
Good pinch of salt
150ml olive oil

Mix together all the marinade ingredients in a large container.

Rub the marinade all over the lamb so it's completely covered.
Cover and marinate in the fridge for a minimum of 4 hours, ideally
overnight.

TO MAKE

✢ ✢ ✢ ✢ ✢ ✢ ✢ ✢ ✢ ✢ ✢ ✢ ✢ ✢ ✢ ✢ ✢ ✢

1.5 – 2kg lamb shoulder, bone in
10 garlic cloves, peeled
4 sprigs of thyme
4 sprigs of rosemary

When you're ready to cook, preheat the oven to 160°C/Fan 140°C/
gas 3.

Take the lamb from the fridge, then get a high-sided oven tray and
line with a layer of foil and a layer of baking paper, large enough
to cover the lamb. Add the garlic and herb sprigs to the middle,
followed by the lamb and all the marinade (you can also add onions,
carrots or potatoes at this stage, if you like). Fold the foil and baking
paper over the lamb like a parcel, then flip it over and wrap it again
in another layer of foil so the lamb is tightly wrapped and there are
no gaps. We want to cook the lamb in its own juices, so it's really
important that it's completely covered at this stage.

Place in the oven and cook for 4 hours or until the meat is falling off
the bone. Remove from the oven, unwrap, increase the temperature
to 200°C/Fan 180°C/gas 6 and roast until browned on top.

TO SERVE

✢ ✢ ✢ ✢ ✢ ✢ ✢ ✢ ✢ ✢ ✢ ✢ ✢ ✢ ✢ ✢ ✢ ✢

Kabsa rice (page 166)
Plain bulgur (page 49) Serve
 with all its juices.

This is best with kabsa rice or plain bulgur.

KEBAB HINDI

Minced lamb koftas in rich tomato sauce

Hindi means 'from India', but this dish isn't from India, it's a Damascene recipe – and the funny thing about it is that in India they have a Chammi kebab (meaning from Damascus, because in the old days it was called Chamma), but it has nothing to do with Damascus! Even with food people are always crossing over and sharing, but in this case the name comes from Indian family coming to settle in Syria a long time ago. This is a classic original recipe which I had nothing to do with creating.

Even at home we don't waste food. We eat it the next day, so we don't worry if we make a lot of this. I prefer the chilli paste hot, but feel free to change it – my wife doesn't really like it hot! If you don't have the chilli paste or don't want to use it, the tomato purée is fine – just use an extra ½ tablespoon. Serve with the green plate (page 45).

Pictured overleaf.

FOR THE TOMATO SAUCE

✤ ✤ ✤ ✤ ✤ ✤ ✤ ✤ ✤ ✤ ✤ ✤ ✤ ✤ ✤ ✤ ✤

2 tablespoons olive oil, plus extra
   to drizzle
1 teaspoon cumin seeds
2 medium onions, diced
2 x 400g tins of chopped tomatoes
1 tablespoon tomato purée
1 tablespoon chilli paste
   (see introduction)

Heat the olive oil for the tomato sauce in a saucepan over a medium heat and add the cumin seeds. Cook, stirring, for 30 – 60 seconds, until the seeds start to pop and toast. Add the onions and cook for 5 – 7 minutes until they soften and caramelise a little, then add the tomatoes. When it starts to simmer, add the tomato purée and chilli paste. Stirring often, cook for 25 – 40 minutes over a medium heat, with the lid on. You will know it's cooked by tasting: it will taste of cooked tomatoes. Take off the heat and let it cool down to room temperature or a little warmer. Pour it into a 30cm roasting tin or dish to help it cool down – we are going to use the roasting tin for the koftas.

Preheat the oven to 200°C/Fan 180°C/gas 6.

FOR THE KOFTAS

✤ ✤ ✤ ✤ ✤ ✤ ✤ ✤ ✤ ✤ ✤ ✤ ✤ ✤ ✤ ✤ ✤

1 medium onion, roughly chopped
2 garlic cloves, peeled
1 teaspoon baharat (page 32)
½ teaspoon flaky sea salt
½ teaspoon coarsely ground
   black pepper
500g minced lamb

In a food processor, blend the onion, garlic, baharat, salt and black pepper to make a paste. Then add the lamb and pulse to combine. Shape the mixture into 20 balls. Squeeze each ball in your hands to make a small kebab shape in your fist. Place on top of the tomato sauce in the roasting tin. Don't worry that the sauce is still quite watery – that's OK. Arrange them close to each other because they will shrink down as they cook in the oven.

Drizzle with a little olive oil and bake in the oven for 30 minutes, to reduce the sauce and cook the kebabs through.

TO SERVE

✤ ✤ ✤ ✤ ✤ ✤ ✤ ✤ ✤ ✤ ✤ ✤ ✤ ✤ ✤ ✤ ✤

Chopped parsley (as much
   as you like, but at least
   ½ handful)
½ handful of toasted pine nuts

To serve, top with chopped parsley and toasted pine nuts.

ZAHRAA HARRA

Cauliflower, red onions, red peppers

FOR THE MARINADE

❖ ❖

5 garlic cloves, minced
2 tablespoons tomato purée
1 tablespoon harissa paste
100ml olive oil

Mix together the marinade ingredients in a small bowl, with a pinch each of salt and black pepper.

If your cauliflower has a lot of leaves, remove the toughest leaves from the outside, leaving the lighter ones attached. Chop the cauliflower into 8 wedges then coat them in three-quarters of the marinade so that all the gaps are coated. At this stage you can marinate them for up to 12 hours, but you can also cook them straight away.

TO MAKE

❖ ❖

1 large cauliflower
1 red onion
2 red romano peppers
1 teaspoon dried or fresh thyme
1 teaspoon sumac
Salt and ground black pepper

Preheat the oven to 200°C/Fan 180°C/gas 6 and line a large low-sided baking tray with baking paper. Add the cauliflower wedges to the lined tray and roast for 15 minutes.

While the cauliflower is roasting, chop the red onion and red peppers into similar-sized pieces (about 3cm) and, in a bowl, coat with the remaining marinade, the thyme and sumac. Remove the cauliflower from the oven and turn each wedge over. Add the onions and peppers to the tray and put back in the oven for a further 25 minutes until the cauliflower is crispy and golden and the onions and peppers are soft.

TO SERVE

❖ ❖

Tahini sauce (page 54)
Coriander oil (page 37)
Aleppo chilli flakes

Serve immediately with a little more salt and pepper, tahini sauce, coriander oil and chilli flakes.

FASULIA BIL ZAYT

Green beans and tomato sauce

This is a great side dish or a vegan/vegetarian main. You can make it in advance, as it's served at room temperature.

TO MAKE

✤ ✤ ✤ ✤ ✤ ✤ ✤ ✤ ✤ ✤ ✤ ✤ ✤ ✤ ✤ ✤ ✤ ✤

450g fine green beans,
  tails trimmed
2 tablespoons olive oil
1 teaspoon cumin seeds
5 garlic cloves, very thinly sliced
1–2 red chillies, very thinly sliced
  (optional)
1 tablespoon tomato purée
1 tablespoon red pepper paste
1 x 400g tin of chopped tomatoes
1 teaspoon ground cumin
1 teaspoon ground black pepper
Good pinch of salt

Boil the beans in a large pot of salted water for 3–4 minutes, until just cooked. Drain and set aside.

In the same pot, over a medium heat, add the olive oil and cumin seeds and toast for a minute before adding the garlic and chillies and frying for a minute. Add the tomato purée and pepper paste, stir to cook out for a few minutes then add the chopped tomatoes. Stir in the ground cumin, pepper and salt, then simmer for 10–15 minutes until you have a thick, rich sauce.

Add the green beans for the last few minutes then turn off the heat and allow to cool to room temperature.

TO SERVE

✤ ✤ ✤ ✤ ✤ ✤ ✤ ✤ ✤ ✤ ✤ ✤ ✤ ✤ ✤ ✤ ✤

Tahini sauce (page 54)
Green plate (page 45)
Greek-style yogurt (optional)

Serve with tahini sauce, a green plate and a dollop of yogurt on the side, if you like.

MAHASHI

Stuffed vine leaves

If you can't find high-fat minced lamb, add 1 tablespoon of ghee.

FOR THE VINE LEAF STUFFING

✧ ✧

200g short-grain Egyptian rice
2 tablespoons safflower
2 teaspoons ground cumin
1 teaspoon ground black pepper
1 teaspoon baharat (page 32)
400g high-fat (30%) minced lamb
50 vine leaves (see introduction
    on page 76)

Wash the rice until the water runs clear then add to a bowl with the safflower and mix thoroughly (wearing gloves to save your hands from going yellow). Add the cumin, black pepper, baharat, minced lamb and a good pinch of salt, then mix again with your hands.

Prepare your vine leaves (see introduction on page 76) then lay one out, ideally on a tray, in front of you. Spoon 1 tablespoon of the rice and lamb mixture into the middle of the leaf. Fold the sides inwards like an envelope, then roll away from you, making a neat little roll. Set aside on another tray and continue with the rest until you have used all the leaves and filling.

FOR THE SAUCE

✧ ✧

Juice of 4 lemons
500ml water
1 whole bulb of garlic, cloves
    peeled and smashed to a paste
1 teaspoon ground black pepper
1 teaspoon baharat (page 32)
1 tablespoon tomato purée
Salt

Add the lemon juice and water to another bowl, then add the garlic, black pepper, baharat, 2 teaspoons of salt and the tomato purée and mix together until combined.

TO MAKE

❖ ❖ ❖ ❖ ❖ ❖ ❖ ❖ ❖ ❖ ❖ ❖ ❖ ❖ ❖ ❖ ❖ ❖ ❖

2 starchy potatoes, peeled and
   cut into 1cm slices
800g lamb neck, sliced into
   2cm pieces (ask your butcher
   to do this)
2 whole garlic bulbs
1 jar of artichoke hearts, drained
   (optional)
Yogurt

In a wide, heavy-based pot or flameproof casserole, 30 – 35cm
diameter, layer the sliced potatoes to completely cover the base.
Now add the lamb neck in a layer, placing the slices so they fit tightly
together. Add the stuffed vine leaves on top of the lamb neck, laying
them tightly around the edge of the dish in concentric rings and
stacking on top of each other, until the final 2 layers where you want
to leave a gap in the middle.

Place the garlic bulbs in the gap in the middle, along with the
artichokes, if using, then place a weight on top of everything.
I have a traditional weight that is meant for this dish, but if you
don't, then stack 3 – 5 plates on top instead, which works fine.

Pour over the sauce to just cover everything; you might not need
all of it, so set aside the rest in case you need to top up later. Tightly
cover the pot with foil or a lid then place over a high heat until the
liquid is boiling. Boil for 10 minutes, then turn the heat down to low
and simmer for 1 hour.

Remove the lid, put a little pressure on the weight or plates, tilt and
carefully drain as much of the liquid as you can into a bowl. Remove
the weight and the garlic bulbs, and artichokes, if using, then place
a serving platter or tray on top of the pot. Very quickly and carefully
flip the pot over so it's upside down on the tray.

Gently lift the pot up, revealing the layers of the potato, meat
and vine leaves.

Place the garlic and artichokes back on the top of the potatoes
and serve with the sauce you saved earlier, and some yogurt.

JAJ BAILFURN

Grilled chicken thighs

This is a staple, midweek, one-tray meal. You can use any vegetables you have in the fridge, too, so it's a great way to use up anything you have.

FOR THE MARINADE

✧ ✧ ✧ ✧ ✧ ✧ ✧ ✧ ✧ ✧ ✧ ✧ ✧ ✧ ✧ ✧ ✧ ✧ ✧

1 teaspoon tomato purée
2 tablespoons shish taouk
　(page 33)
1 teaspoon mild Madras
　curry powder
5 garlic cloves, crushed
1 tablespoon ground black pepper
2 tablespoons Greek-style yogurt
Good pinch of salt
2 tablespoons white wine vinegar
100ml olive oil

In a bowl, mix together all the marinade ingredients, adding the oil last. Take out 2 tablespoons and set aside for later.

TO MAKE

✧ ✧ ✧ ✧ ✧ ✧ ✧ ✧ ✧ ✧ ✧ ✧ ✧ ✧ ✧ ✧ ✧ ✧

8 chicken thighs, skin on and
　bone in
2 carrots, chopped into
　5cm chunks
2 large floury potatoes,
　chopped into 5cm chunks
1 onion, peeled and cut into
　6 wedges
150g baby chestnut mushrooms

Add the chicken to the marinade and mix well so the pieces are all evenly coated. Cover and marinate in the fridge for a minimum of 2 hours, ideally overnight.

When you're ready to cook, preheat the oven to 200°C/Fan 180°C/gas 6 and remove the chicken from the fridge.

Add all the vegetables to a large, high-sided oven tray. Place the chicken thighs on top, skin side up, wrap the tray tightly in foil and cook for 25 minutes, then remove from the oven, remove the foil and brush the chicken with the reserved marinade. Return to the oven for a further 20 minutes until the chicken skin is crispy. You may need to turn up your oven here to get a crispy skin.

TO SERVE

✧ ✧ ✧ ✧ ✧ ✧ ✧ ✧ ✧ ✧ ✧ ✧ ✧ ✧ ✧ ✧ ✧ ✧

Rice or tabbouleh (page 100)

Serve immediately with rice or tabbouleh.

SYRIAN FISH AND CHIPS WITH TAHINI SAUCE

FOR THE FISH

✦ ✦ ✦ ✦ ✦ ✦ ✦ ✦ ✦ ✦ ✦ ✦ ✦ ✦ ✦ ✦ ✦ ✦

4 haddock fillets
2 teaspoons ground cumin
1 teaspoon ground white pepper
4 garlic cloves, crushed
50ml olive oil
200g plain flour
1 tablespoon cornflour
Salt

Put the haddock in a dish. In a bowl, mix the cumin, white pepper, garlic, olive oil and a pinch of salt. Pour this over the fish, cover and leave to marinate in the fridge for at least 4 hours, or overnight.

FOR THE TAHINI SAUCE

✦ ✦ ✦ ✦ ✦ ✦ ✦ ✦ ✦ ✦ ✦ ✦ ✦ ✦ ✦ ✦ ✦ ✦

50g tahini
1 garlic clove, crushed
Juice of 1 lemon
Small handful of parsley, chopped
1 tablespoon ice-cold water

Meanwhile, make the tahini sauce. In a bowl, mix together the tahini, garlic, lemon juice and chopped parsley. Stir in the ice-cold water until you have a creamy sauce, then set aside.

FOR THE CHIPS

✦ ✦ ✦ ✦ ✦ ✦ ✦ ✦ ✦ ✦ ✦ ✦ ✦ ✦ ✦ ✦ ✦ ✦

800g potatoes, ideally Maris
  Piper or King Edward
2 litres sunflower or vegetable oil
1 teaspoon smoked paprika

For the chips, peel and cut the potatoes into finger-thick chips (about 1cm). Pour the oil into a large, heavy-based pot (it should be at least 9cm deep, but not over halfway up your pot). Place over a medium-high heat until it reaches 140°C (if you don't have a thermometer, add a small piece of potato to the oil and if it floats to the top and fries, you're good to go). Add the chips in small batches and fry for around 8 minutes until very lightly golden and mostly cooked, removing with a slotted spoon to kitchen paper.

Turn up the heat slightly (if you have a thermometer, you want it to be at 180°C, or you can test with a chip again; it should turn golden much faster than the first time). Add your chips in batches again, and fry for 2–3 minutes until golden, removing to new kitchen paper. Season generously with salt and paprika.

Return to the fish: put the flour, a pinch of salt and the cornflour in a bowl and mix. Dip the fish pieces in the flour one by one until completely covered with flour. Make sure the oil is still at 180°C, then fry the fish pieces for 5–6 minutes until they turn golden and crispy. Serve with the chips and the tahini sauce.

MUJADARA

Bulgur wheat with brown lentils

SERVES 4–6

This is nice either hot or cold, so it's great to make extra and eat the next day as a salad. Use the best extra virgin olive oil you have, as your whole dish will taste of it.

TO MAKE

❖ ❖ ❖ ❖ ❖ ❖ ❖ ❖ ❖ ❖ ❖ ❖ ❖ ❖ ❖ ❖ ❖ ❖

200g dried brown lentils
100ml extra virgin olive oil
1 tablespoon cumin seeds
1 large onion, finely chopped
1 teaspoon ground black pepper
1 teaspoon baharat (page 32)
1 teaspoon mild Madras
  curry powder
200g coarse bulgur wheat
Salt

Wash the lentils in a sieve until the water runs clear.

Add 75ml of the olive oil to a medium saucepan with the cumin seeds over a medium-high heat and toast for a minute, then turn down the heat a little, add the onion and cook for 8–10 minutes until soft and slightly caramelised.

Tip in the lentils with 1 teaspoon of salt, then add the spices and stir to toast and coat the lentils with the oil. Add water to come about 3cm above the lentils, then cover with a lid and bring to the boil. Lower to a bubbling simmer for 20 minutes until almost cooked; you want the lentils to still be a little firm.

Now stir in the bulgur wheat plus the remaining olive oil. Top up the water if necessary so it is still 3cm above the lentils and bulgur, using boiling water. Cover and turn up the heat to a boil for 3–5 minutes, then take off the heat. Cover the whole pot with a clean tea towel and set aside for 30–45 minutes.

TO SERVE

❖ ❖ ❖ ❖ ❖ ❖ ❖ ❖ ❖ ❖ ❖ ❖ ❖ ❖ ❖ ❖ ❖ ❖

Crispy onions (page 54)
Green plate (page 45)
Pickled cucumbers (page 56)
Turkish pickled peppers
Laban bikhiar (page 97)

Remove the tea towel and lid then break up the grains with a fork and taste for seasoning. Serve topped with crispy onions and your favourite sides.

MUJADARA SALAD

TO MAKE

✧ ✧ ✧ ✧ ✧ ✧ ✧ ✧ ✧ ✧ ✧ ✧ ✧ ✧ ✧ ✧ ✧ ✧

300g leftover mujadara
  (see page 158)
3 baby cucumbers, finely diced
6 radishes, finely sliced
Handful of parsley,
  roughly chopped
Small handful of mint leaves,
  roughly chopped
50g pine nuts, toasted
1 large beef tomato, deseeded
  and finely chopped
Juice of 1 lemon
50ml extra virgin olive oil
Flaky sea salt and ground
  black pepper

Add everything to a large serving bowl, with salt and pepper to taste, and toss together to combine.

KABSA RICE
WITH PRAWNS

TO MAKE

✦ ✦

2 tablespoons olive oil

1 tablespoon cumin seeds

3 cloves

1 cinnamon stick

3 green cardamom pods

1½ tablespoons kabsa spice
   (page 32)

1 teaspoon ground black pepper

1½ teaspoons baharat (page 32)

1 bay leaf

1 large onion, finely chopped

1 green pepper, deseeded and
   finely chopped

1 or 2 small red chillies
   (optional)

1 x 400g tin of tomatoes

2 teaspoons salt

400g American long-grain rice
   (or other long-grain rice)

75g golden raisins or sultanas

300g peeled raw king prawns

Heat the olive oil in a large, heavy-based pan over a medium-high heat then add the cumin seeds and toast for a minute. Add all the remaining spices and bay leaf and cook for a further minute, stirring continuously. Add the onion and green pepper and fry for 10 minutes until soft, stirring regularly and turning the heat down if needed to ensure the spices don't catch. If you want to add a chilli or two, slice in half lengthways and add to the pot.

Add the tomatoes and salt, then fill the empty tomato tin with water and pour it in. Bring everything to the boil then turn down to a simmer for 25 minutes.

Meanwhile, wash the rice in a sieve until the water runs clear, then add to a bowl with enough water to cover. Soak for 30 minutes.

Taste the sauce at this point, making sure the seasoning is right, then drain the rice and stir it into the pan, along with the raisins and prawns, making sure you have about 2cm of liquid above the rice; if not, add a little more water.

Bring the rice back up to the boil, then put the lid on and immediately turn it right down to the lowest simmer for 15 minutes. Take off the heat, leaving the lid tightly on, and rest for 10 minutes.

TO SERVE

✦ ✦ ✦ ✦ ✦ ✦ ✦ ✦ ✦ ✦ ✦ ✦ ✦ ✦ ✦ ✦ ✦ ✦

50g pine nuts, toasted

Handful of chopped parsley

Laban bikhiar (page 97)

Green salad

Lift the lid on the rice and stir it gently with a fork to break up the grains, then serve with the pine nuts, parsley, laban bikhiar and a green salad.

KABSA RICE
WITH CHICKEN

TO MAKE

✦ ✦ ✦ ✦ ✦ ✦ ✦ ✦ ✦ ✦ ✦ ✦ ✦ ✦ ✦ ✦ ✦ ✦ ✦

2 tablespoons olive oil

4 chicken legs

1 tablespoon cumin seeds

3 cloves

1 cinnamon stick

3 green cardamom pods

1½ tablespoons kabsa spice
   (page 32)

1½ teaspoons baharat (page 32)

1 teaspoon ground black pepper

1 bay leaf

1 large onion, finely chopped

1 green pepper, deseeded and
   finely chopped

1 or 2 small red chillies (optional)

1 x 400g tin of tomatoes

2 teaspoons salt

400g American long-grain rice
   (or other long-grain rice)

75g golden raisins or sultanas

Heat the olive oil in a large, heavy-based pan over a medium-high heat, add the chicken legs skin side down and brown for about 7 minutes (you may need to do this in 2 batches). Remove and set aside on a plate.

Add the cumin seeds to the same pan and toast for a minute then add all the remaining spices and the bay leaf, and cook for a further minute, stirring continuously. Add the onion and green pepper and fry for 10 minutes until soft, stirring regularly and turning the heat down if needed to ensure the spices don't catch. If you want to add a chilli or two, slice in half lengthways and add to the pan.

Add the tomatoes and salt, fill the empty tomato tin with water and pour it in, then bring everything up to the boil. Add the chicken back in, making sure it's completely submerged in the sauce; if it's not, just top up with a little more water. Put the lid on and turn down to a bubbling simmer for 45 minutes.

Meanwhile, wash the rice in a sieve until the water runs clear, then add to a bowl with enough water to cover. Soak for 30 minutes.

Preheat the oven on the grill setting.

Remove the chicken from the pan to a low-sided roasting tray. Taste the sauce at this point, making sure the seasoning is right.

Drain the rice and stir it into the pot along with the raisins, making sure you have about 2cm of liquid above the rice; if not add a little more water in.

Bring the rice back up to the boil, then put the lid on and immediately turn it right down to the lowest simmer for 15 minutes. Take off the heat, leaving the lid tightly on, and rest for 10 minutes.

While the rice is resting, place the chicken under the grill for 5–10 minutes until the skin crisps up again and is golden.

TO SERVE

✦ ✦ ✦ ✦ ✦ ✦ ✦ ✦ ✦ ✦ ✦ ✦ ✦ ✦ ✦ ✦ ✦ ✦

Shelled pistachios (optional)
50g pine nuts, toasted
Handful of chopped parsley
Laban bikhiar (page 97)
Green salad

Lift the lid on the rice and stir it gently with a fork to break up the grains, then serve with the chicken, pistchios, if using, pine nuts, parsley, laban bikhiar and a green salad.

KABSA RICE WITH VEGETABLES

TO MAKE

❖ ❖ ❖ ❖ ❖ ❖ ❖ ❖ ❖ ❖ ❖ ❖ ❖ ❖ ❖ ❖ ❖ ❖ ❖

4 tablespoons olive oil
1 tablespoon cumin seeds
250g chestnut mushrooms, sliced
3 red peppers, deseeded and
   roughly chopped
1 green pepper, deseeded
   and finely chopped
2 red onions, cut into
   slices 1cm thick
1 or 2 small red chillies
   (optional)
1½ tablespoons kabsa spice
   (page 32)
1 teaspoon ground black pepper
1½ teaspoons baharat (page 32)
3 cloves
1 cinnamon stick
3 green cardamom pods
1 bay leaf
2 teaspoons salt
1 x 400g tin of tomatoes
400g American long-grain rice
   (or other long-grain rice)
75g golden raisins or sultanas

Heat 2 tablespoons of the olive oil in a large heavy-based pan over a medium-high heat, then add the cumin seeds and toast for a minute, followed by the sliced mushrooms. Cook over a high heat for 4 – 5 minutes, stirring occasionally. Remove from the pan once they are nice and golden and set aside on a plate.

Add the remaining olive oil to the pan and cook the peppers and red onions for 8 – 10 minutes, to get a little colour. If you want to add a chilli or two, slice in half lengthways and add to the pot. Return the mushrooms to the pan with spices and salt. Fry for 2 – 3 minutes then add the tomatoes.

Fill the empty tomato tin with water and add it in, then bring everything up to the boil. Put the lid on and turn down to a bubbling simmer for 25 – 30 minutes.

Meanwhile, wash the rice in a sieve until the water runs clear, then add to a bowl with enough water to cover. Soak for 30 minutes.

Taste the sauce at this point, making sure the seasoning is right, then drain the rice and stir it into the pan along with the raisins.

Bring the rice back up to the boil, then put the lid on and immediately turn it right down to the lowest simmer for 15 minutes. Take off the heat, leaving the lid tightly on, and rest for 10 minutes.

TO SERVE

❖ ❖ ❖ ❖ ❖ ❖ ❖ ❖ ❖ ❖ ❖ ❖ ❖ ❖ ❖ ❖ ❖ ❖

Laban bikhiar (page 97)
50g pine nuts, toasted
Handful of chopped parsley
Green salad

Lift the lid on the rice and stir it gently with a fork to break up the grains, then serve with the laban bikhiar, pine nuts, parsley, and a green salad.

STUFFED COURGETTES, AUBERGINES AND PEPPERS

If you can't find high-fat minced lamb, add 1 tablespoon of ghee.

PREPARE THE VEGETABLES

✧ ✧ ✧ ✧ ✧ ✧ ✧ ✧ ✧ ✧ ✧ ✧ ✧ ✧ ✧ ✧ ✧ ✧ ✧

5 baby aubergines
10 baby courgettes
4 peppers
Salt and ground black pepper

Core the aubergines and courgettes so you have a hole down the middle to stuff, then remove the stems from the peppers to reveal a hole, also for stuffing. Keep the stems to use as lids.

FOR THE FILLING

✧ ✧ ✧ ✧ ✧ ✧ ✧ ✧ ✧ ✧ ✧ ✧ ✧ ✧ ✧ ✧ ✧ ✧

200g short-grain Egyptian rice
2 tablespoons safflower
2 teaspoons ground cumin
1 teaspoon baharat (page 32)
400g high-fat (30%)
  minced lamb

For the filling, wash the rice until the water runs clear then add to a bowl with the safflower and mix thoroughly (wearing gloves to save your hands from going yellow). Add the cumin, baharat, minced lamb, a good pinch of salt and 1 teaspoon of black pepper, then mix again with your hands.

FOR THE SAUCE

✧ ✧ ✧ ✧ ✧ ✧ ✧ ✧ ✧ ✧ ✧ ✧ ✧ ✧ ✧ ✧ ✧ ✧ ✧

Juice of 1 lemon
200ml tamarind sauce (page 130)
10 garlic cloves, smashed into
  a paste
1 teaspoon baharat (page 32)
1 tablespoon safflower
2 tablespoons tomato purée

For the sauce, add the lemon juice, tamarind sauce, garlic, baharat, safflower, tomato purée, a good pinch of salt and 1 teaspoon of black pepper to another bowl, and mix together until combined.

Stuff the cavities in the vegetables until three-quarters full then stand them upright in a deep, 30cm diameter, heavy-based pot or flameproof casserole, so they are tightly packed.

Pour over the sauce to just cover everything; you might not need all of it, so set aside the rest in case you need to top up later. Tightly cover with foil or a lid and place over a high heat until the liquid is boiling. Boil for 10 minutes, then turn the heat down to low and simmer for 1 hour before serving.

MY JOURNEY TO THE UK, PART 2

SO, HOW DID I FINALLY make it to the UK? I told the Home Office it was in the back of a lorry, but the truth is I came with a fake ID on a first-class Eurostar ticket from Paris to London.

After the failure of the flights to Heathrow, I asked my contact for a new passport. This time he sent a genuine passport, but it wasn't my face on the photo. It was a man who looked only a little like me, but it would be good enough. I hoped. I didn't want to leave anything else to chance, I wanted to take control of the situation, so I decided I'd book my own ticket. There was no way I was going back to the airport so I headed to the train station. I'd take the Eurostar to London. When I got to Gare du Nord, it was early evening, rush hour, and there were no regular tickets left, only first class. It was expensive, €182, almost all the money I had left, but by then I had psyched myself up, I was ready. I was leaving tonight, no more waiting around. I bought the ticket and headed to security.

I swear I was visibly shaking as I approached French passport control. I handed my papers over and the officer looked at them, and then looked at me. And I could see at once in his eyes that he knew. He didn't believe the man in the photo was me, but he waved me through anyway. I didn't understand why, was it another miracle? But then I saw. Ahead of me was another checkpoint, the British one. I was shocked to see it, I didn't know they were both this side of the train. And I was so, so scared. Standing in the queue, trying to figure out the situation and look calm, while panic was building inside me. The British passport officer was questioning the woman in front. Really interrogating her. Why was she in Paris? Why was she travelling alone? Where was she going in the UK? How long for? She was the most English-looking person I'd ever seen. If he was asking her so many questions, how was he going to react when it was my turn? Syrian, physically worn down after months on the road, with my smuggler's fake ID? Their voices continued to rise along with my anxiety, but then the woman suddenly exploded, screaming and swearing until security pulled her away. Now it was me.

I walked over to the desk and slid my ticket and passport under the glass. Behind the screen, the officer was talking to his colleague in the next booth, explaining what had just happened, still worked up from the woman's reaction. He scanned my passport in his machine without even looking at it, or me. In fact, he hadn't said a word to me at all. He was totally ignoring me. I thought to myself: what would a British person do? What would a British person, holding a first-class ticket do? I said 'Excuse me, I haven't got all day.' Surprised and flustered he handed me back my papers and said, 'I'm so sorry, Sir. Have a good trip'. And I was through. I took a few steps, then had to stoop down to re-tie my shoelace because I thought I might faint. I was blocking the path, so a security guard asked me to please move somewhere else. So I walked with my bag to first class.

Arriving into the late evening air in London I felt myself relax for the first time in so long. I called my sister in Doncaster and she was jumping for joy. I let my family know I was safe. Then I hung around the station until 4am, bought a ticket to Doncaster and stayed with my sister and brother-in-law and their kids that first night. In the morning I'd go to the Home Office to start the process of becoming a UK citizen.

BUTTERED HALIBUT

A beloved, traditional dish in Syria that's very popular in the summer, this recipe is particularly appreciated on the Mediterranean seaside. This dish is a real crowd-pleaser because of its simplicity; the sauce is only here to enhance the flavour of the halibut and the lemon brings enough acidity and freshness without overpowering it.

TO MAKE

✦ ✦ ✦ ✦ ✦ ✦ ✦ ✦ ✦ ✦ ✦ ✦ ✦ ✦ ✦ ✦ ✦ ✦

50g butter
2 garlic cloves, crushed
1 teaspoon cumin seeds
1 teaspoon salt
½ teaspoon ground black pepper
4 x 200g halibut fillets
1 lemon, thinly sliced
Sprinkle of fresh thyme leaves
Sprinkle of sumac
Sprinkle of Aleppo chilli flakes

Preheat the oven to 180°C/Fan 160°C/gas 4.

In a small saucepan, melt the butter over a medium-low heat. Once melted, add the garlic, cumin, salt and pepper, and stir to combine.

Put the fish fillets in an ovenproof dish and pour over the butter mixture. Lay the lemon slices on top and cover the dish with foil. Bake for 5–8 minutes, depending on the thickness of the fillets, then remove the foil and bake for another 5 minutes until the fish flakes easily with a fork.

Sprinkle with a little thyme, sumac and chilli flakes and serve.

KUFTAH TAHINI

This recipe needs a high-fat mince, and works well with just lamb or just beef mince too, if you didn't want to do a mix.

Pictured overleaf.

FOR THE SAUCE

❖ ❖ ❖ ❖ ❖ ❖ ❖ ❖ ❖ ❖ ❖ ❖ ❖ ❖ ❖ ❖

1 onion, roughly chopped
3 garlic cloves, peeled
Small handful of parsley, stalks and leaves separated
1 tablespoon red pepper paste

For the sauce, in a blender, blitz the onion, garlic, parsley stalks (reserve and chop the leaves for serving) and red pepper paste until smooth.

TO MAKE

❖ ❖ ❖ ❖ ❖ ❖ ❖ ❖ ❖ ❖ ❖ ❖ ❖ ❖ ❖ ❖

750g minced beef (15–20% fat)
250g minced lamb (15–20% fat)
2 tablespoons Greek-style yogurt
2 tablespoons pomegranate molasses
1 teaspoon ground black pepper
1 teaspoon baharat (page 32)
½ teaspoon ground coriander
½ teaspoon ground cumin
2 teaspoons salt

Preheat the oven to 220°C/Fan 200°C/gas 7.

Add the minced meats to a mixing bowl with the blended sauce, yogurt, pomegranate molasses, black pepper, baharat, ground coriander, cumin and salt. Mix well with your hands until everything is combined.

Add the spiced mince to a 30cm round baking tin or ovenproof frying pan, and pat down with your hands into an even layer. With your fingertips, press down around the edges of the tin or pan to separate the mixture from the edges of the tin or pan a little. Again, with your fingertips, dimple the surface all over.

FOR THE GARNISH

❖ ❖ ❖ ❖ ❖ ❖ ❖ ❖ ❖ ❖ ❖ ❖ ❖ ❖ ❖ ❖ ❖

1 large tomato, cut into 6 wedges
1 red onion, cut into slices 1cm thick
2 – 3 red chillies, halved
   lengthways (optional)
1 teaspoon dried rosemary
1 tablespoon olive oil
Salt and ground black pepper

Arrange the fresh tomato wedges, red onion, chillies, if using, and dried rosemary on top, then drizzle with the olive oil and season with salt and pepper.

Bake in the oven for 30 minutes until crispy and golden on top. If there is any water that has come from the meat, drain off and return to the oven to finish.

TO SERVE

❖ ❖ ❖ ❖ ❖ ❖ ❖ ❖ ❖ ❖ ❖ ❖ ❖ ❖ ❖ ❖ ❖

5 tablespoons tahini sauce
   (page 54)
Chilli oil (optional)
Pitta bread
Green plate (page 45)

While it is still hot, drizzle over the tahini sauce and chilli oil, if using, and serve with the reserved chopped parsley leaves, pitta bread and green plate. I also love it in a pitta bread, like a sandwich.

KUFTAH BETINJAN

FOR THE TOMATO SAUCE

✧ ✧ ✧ ✧ ✧ ✧ ✧ ✧ ✧ ✧ ✧ ✧ ✧ ✧ ✧ ✧ ✧ ✧

1 x 400g tin of tomatoes
1 tablespoon tomato purée
100g tamarind sauce (page 130)
1 garlic clove, peeled
½ teaspoon ground coriander
½ teaspoon ground cumin
1 teaspoon baharat (page 32)
½ teaspoon salt
1 teaspoon ground black pepper

In a food processor, blitz all the ingredients for the tomato sauce together, then pour into a large bowl and set aside.

TO MAKE

✧ ✧ ✧ ✧ ✧ ✧ ✧ ✧ ✧ ✧ ✧ ✧ ✧ ✧ ✧ ✧ ✧ ✧

1 onion, roughly chopped
1 small tomato, halved
600g minced lamb
1 teaspoon baharat (page 32)
½ teaspoon salt
½ teaspoon ground black pepper
6 baby aubergines,
  or 1–2 medium-sized
1 red onion, peeled
2 large beef tomatoes

In the same food processor (wash it first), blitz the onion and tomato and add it to another mixing bowl with the minced lamb, baharat, salt and pepper. Use your hands to mix well to combine, then roll the mixture into 25g balls (about the size of a large walnut). Lightly flatten into discs.

Preheat the oven 200°C/Fan 180°C/gas 6.

Slice the aubergines 1cm thick (if using larger aubergines, cut them in half lengthways first). Cut the onion in half through the root and the tomato in half through the core. Cut each halved vegetable into half-moon slices 1cm thick. Arrange the lamb discs and the vegetables (skin side up) in an oven dish, about 25 x 32cm, alternating them as you go.

Pour over the tomato sauce then cover the dish with foil and bake in the oven for 20 minutes. Remove the foil and return to the oven for 25 minutes until the lamb is golden on top and the aubergines are soft.

TO SERVE

✧ ✧ ✧ ✧ ✧ ✧ ✧ ✧ ✧ ✧ ✧ ✧ ✧ ✧ ✧ ✧ ✧ ✧

Juice of 1 lemon
Chopped parsley
Rice or bulgur wheat
Green plate (page 45)

Squeeze the lemon juice on top and scatter with parsley to finish, then serve with rice or bulgur wheat and a green plate.

MANZILAT BETINJAN

Baked aubergines and lamb

This is ideally made with baby aubergines, but I've adapted it here to use the larger ones. If you can find baby ones, I'd recommend using those instead – 6–8.

TO MAKE

✦ ✦ ✦ ✦ ✦ ✦ ✦ ✦ ✦ ✦ ✦ ✦ ✦ ✦ ✦ ✦ ✦ ✦

3 aubergines
4–5 tablespoons olive oil
1 tablespoon cumin seeds
1 teaspoon baharat (page 32)
1 tablespoon ground black pepper
2 small onions, finely chopped
1 tablespoon tomato purée
500g minced lamb (15–20% fat)
3 large beef or vine tomatoes
  (the best, reddest ones you
  can get), sliced
2 green peppers
  (ideally Turkish ones but you
  can use bell peppers), deseeded
  and finely sliced
Salt

Using a swivel vegetable peeler, peel off the skin from the aubergines in vertical stripes, so you're left with some skin on; this will give it a little more smoky taste. Now cut them across into round slices 1cm thick and place in a single layer on a few baking trays. Salt them generously then lay over some kitchen paper to soak up the moisture that will come out of them – this will take about 10 minutes. Replace the damp kitchen paper with new sheets to remove as much moisture as you can, patting them down. This is important as you want your aubergines to be as dry as possible.

Preheat the oven to 200°C/Fan 180°C/gas 6.

Rub 2–3 tablespoons of olive oil all over the now dry aubergine slices, then roast in the oven for 15–20 minutes until golden on top and slightly softened.

Meanwhile, add 2 tablespoons of olive oil to a large saucepan over a medium heat. Add the cumin seeds, baharat, black pepper and salt to taste and cook for a minute, then add the onions and gently fry for 5 minutes until beginning to soften. Now add the tomato purée and minced lamb and stir for 5 minutes. Remove the aubergines from the oven and layer them into a baking dish, 30 x 20cm. Spoon over the lamb, then lay on the sliced tomatoes, followed by the peppers. Place back in the oven for 20 minutes until slightly crisp on top.

TO SERVE

✦ ✦ ✦ ✦ ✦ ✦ ✦ ✦ ✦ ✦ ✦ ✦ ✦ ✦ ✦ ✦ ✦

Plain rice
Green plate (page 45)

Serve straight away with plain rice and a green plate.

TABAKH ROHO

SERVES 4

Tabakh roho means 'to cook by itself' in Arabic. This makes a lot of delicious lamb stock; allow the leftover stock to cool completely and then store in the fridge for up to 4 days, or in the freezer for 3 months.

FOR THE LAMB

❖ ❖ ❖ ❖ ❖ ❖ ❖ ❖ ❖ ❖ ❖ ❖ ❖ ❖ ❖ ❖ ❖

4 lamb shanks
Choose any 2 – 3 herbs and
  spices from: fresh rosemary,
  fresh or dried bay leaves,
  fresh thyme, cloves, cardamom
  pods, cinnamon stick
1 whole garlic bulb, halved
  horizontally

Place the lamb shanks, chosen herbs and spices and halved garlic bulb in a large pot and add enough water to cover everything. Bring to the boil, scooping off any scum that comes to the surface. Cover with a lid then turn down the heat to a low simmer for 1½ – 2 hours until the meat is about to fall off the bone (the longer you cook it, the more delicious it will be, so feel free to carry on for a little longer). Take off the heat, remove the shanks to a large bowl and keep the lamb stock that's left over for later.

FOR THE SAUCE

❖ ❖ ❖ ❖ ❖ ❖ ❖ ❖ ❖ ❖ ❖ ❖ ❖ ❖ ❖ ❖ ❖

2 tablespoons olive oil
2 teaspoons cumin seeds
2 onions, roughly chopped
1 aubergine, peeled and
  cut into 3cm cubes
4 courgettes, cut into 2cm cubes
1 x 400g tin of chopped tomatoes
1 tablespoon tomato purée
100ml tamarind sauce (page 130)
2 teaspoons baharat (page 32)
1 teaspoon ground black pepper
5 garlic cloves, crushed to a paste
3 teaspoons dried mint
Salt

Add the olive oil to another pot over a medium heat, then add the cumin seeds and toast for a minute before adding the onions, and salt to taste. Stir and cook for a few minutes, then add the aubergine cubes on top of the onions – do not stir!

Turn down the heat to low, cover and allow everything to steam for 10 minutes before adding the courgettes – again, without stirring. Cover again and continue to cook for 10 minutes. Now add the chopped tomatoes, tomato purée, tamarind sauce, 100ml of the reserved lamb stock, the baharat, black pepper and salt to taste.

Gently stir all your layers together and nestle in the lamb shanks. Add the crushed garlic to a small bowl with a few spoonfuls of the sauce and mix together, then add this to the pot. Simmer for 10 – 15 minutes, adding the dried mint for the last 5 minutes.

TO SERVE

❖ ❖ ❖ ❖ ❖ ❖ ❖ ❖ ❖ ❖ ❖ ❖ ❖ ❖ ❖ ❖ ❖

Plain bulgur
Green plate (page 45)

Serve with plain bulgur and a green plate.

KIPPEH

Flat and baked

TO MAKE

✧ ✧ ✧ ✧ ✧ ✧ ✧ ✧ ✧ ✧ ✧ ✧ ✧ ✧ ✧ ✧ ✧ ✧ ✧

2 tablespoons olive oil
1 teaspoon cumin seeds
2 small onions, finely diced
150g minced lamb
2 teaspoons salt
2 teaspoons ground black pepper
2 teaspoons baharat (page 32)
50g toasted pine nuts
150g low-fat (5%) minced beef
Grated zest of ½ lemon
200g fine bulgur wheat,
   rinsed and drained
2 tablespoons melted ghee
1 teaspoon safflower (optional)

Preheat the oven to 180°C/Fan 160°C/gas 4.

Heat the olive oil in a frying pan over a medium heat, add the cumin seeds and toast for 30 seconds. Add half the onion and fry for 5–7 minutes or until softened but not coloured. Add the minced lamb and 1 teaspoon each of the salt, pepper and baharat and fry for 4–5 minutes. Once the meat is cooked, add the pine nuts, remove from the heat and put to one side to cool.

Add the remaining onion to a meat mincer or food processor with the minced beef, lemon zest and remaining salt, pepper and baharat and blitz. Thoroughly drain the bulgur wheat and add to the mincer or processor and blitz again until smooth; you want the paste to be as smooth as possible with no visible onion or bulgur. If necessary, add a tablespoon of water to help combine, then blitz.

Brush a 20cm square baking tin or tray with melted ghee. Add half the beef mixture to cover the base of the tin and pat down with the back of a spoon or spatula until flattened. Tip the lamb mixture in an even layer on top of the beef, followed by the remaining beef mixture. Smooth the top then cut into 16 squares. Brush the top with the remaining ghee, sprinkle with safflower, if using, and bake for 35–40 minutes until browning on top.

TO SERVE

✧ ✧ ✧ ✧ ✧ ✧ ✧ ✧ ✧ ✧ ✧ ✧ ✧ ✧ ✧ ✧ ✧ ✧

Green plate (page 45)

Serve straight away, with a green plate.

KIPPEH MEQLIA

Rolled and fried

TO MAKE

❖ ❖ ❖ ❖ ❖ ❖ ❖ ❖ ❖ ❖ ❖ ❖ ❖ ❖ ❖ ❖ ❖ ❖ ❖

1 quantity of beef and lamb
   kippeh mixtures (page 182)
1 litre vegetable oil,
   for deep-frying

Prepare the lamb and beef and bulgur mixtures as directed on page 182.

Roll the bulgur mixture into large golf-ball-sized balls, then, wetting your thumb and palm a little, make a dent in the middle of each ball using your thumb. Now, with the ball in one hand, work your way around the edges of the hole to start to make it larger, turning as you go to form a cup. You might find it easier to use both index fingers here. Have a little bowl of water ready and remember to wet your hands as you go, as this will stop everything from sticking. The thinner you can get the shell, the better. But it will take practice, so keep going.

Once your little cup is ready, add a small tablespoon of the lamb mixture inside. Then, holding the ball in one hand, seal up the top into a rugby ball shape, making sure there are no gaps. They don't have to be a perfect shape, just well sealed so that when you fry, no filling comes out. Repeat with all the remaining balls.

Heat the oil in a heavy-based saucepan, making sure it comes no more than halfway up the sides of the pan, and heat to 180°C (test it is ready by dropping a little of the mixture into the oil; if it floats and bubbles, then you are ready to go). Deep-fry the kippeh in small batches for 3–4 minutes, turning so they are golden brown all over. Drain on kitchen paper.

TO SERVE

❖ ❖ ❖ ❖ ❖ ❖ ❖ ❖ ❖ ❖ ❖ ❖ ❖ ❖ ❖ ❖ ❖ ❖ ❖

Green plate (page 45)

Serve immediately, with a green plate.

MAKLOUBEH

Lamb and rice

If your butcher can't give you finely diced lamb shoulder, then minced lamb works fine here.

TO MAKE

❖ ❖ ❖ ❖ ❖ ❖ ❖ ❖ ❖ ❖ ❖ ❖ ❖ ❖ ❖ ❖ ❖ ❖ ❖

350g long-grain rice
3 large aubergines, sliced
   lengthways 1cm thick
2 tablespoons olive oil
1 tablespoon ghee
1 teaspoon cumin seeds
350g finely diced lamb shoulder
   (get your butcher to do this)
1½ teaspoons baharat (page 32)
650ml water
Salt and ground black pepper

Preheat the oven to 200°C/Fan 180°C/gas 6.

Wash the rice until the water runs clear, then soak in a bowl of cold water for 30 minutes.

Meanwhile, lay the aubergine slices over a few baking trays in a single layer. Brush each slice with olive oil and sprinkle over a good pinch each of salt and pepper. Roast in the oven for 15 – 20 minutes until soft and lightly golden, then remove and allow to cool slightly.

Add the ghee and cumin seeds to a large 23cm pot and toast for a minute over a medium-high heat. Now add the lamb to brown for 5 minutes. Add ½ teaspoon each of salt and pepper and ½ teaspoon of the baharat. Stir to coat the lamb in the spices, then pat it down so it's all in one layer. Take off the heat and let it cool a little.

Layer the roasted aubergine over the top of the lamb, with half the slices folded up the sides of the pot to line it, so the sides are completely covered (you're building a wall for the rice to cook inside).

Measure out the water into a jug and stir in the remaining teaspoon of baharat, 1 teaspoon of salt and ½ teaspoon of black pepper.

Drain the rice then add to the pot lined with aubergines. Flatten the rice into an even layer with the back of a spoon, then carefully pour the water into the spoon to direct the water gently, into the edges of the pot so that you don't disturb the layers.

Bring everything up to a slow boil with a lid on over a medium heat, then turn down to the lowest heat you can and cook for 15 minutes. Take off the heat and leave to rest for 10 minutes.

TO SERVE

❖ ❖ ❖ ❖ ❖ ❖ ❖ ❖ ❖ ❖ ❖ ❖ ❖ ❖ ❖ ❖ ❖ ❖

Toasted pine nuts
Laban bikhiar (page 97)
Green salad
Small handful of parsley
   and/or mint leaves

To serve, remove the lid and place a large serving plate on top of the pot, then carefully but confidently flip the pot over and lift it little by little to reveal. Scatter over the pine nuts.

Serve with laban bikhiar, green salad and fresh herbs.

FROM REFUGEE TO UK CITIZEN

Being a refugee is exhausting. It's emotional. It's depressing. It involves so much waiting, unable to do anything, completely at the mercy of a constantly changing series of people who mostly don't seem to care. You rely on other people in a way you haven't had to before. You're totally powerless. Even the people involved in the process don't seem to understand the process, and in many ways it's not their fault because it truly makes no sense. There doesn't seem to be any logic to how any of it works.

The day after I arrived in the UK, I walked into the Home Office in Leeds and simply said 'Hello, I'm a Syrian refugee. I came here illegally; will you please take me in?' The man behind the desk gave me a phone number to call. It was all so incredibly routine for them, no one seemed surprised I was there. The woman I spoke to on the phone took my number and I gave her my brother-in-law's number too. She asked if I had somewhere to stay and I said I was staying with family. She then said they'd be in touch about the next steps in getting my status as an asylum seeker approved. And that was it.

After that initial brief phone conversation in Leeds, it was 27 days until I was contacted again. And in that time, no one checked my background, they didn't verify any of my details, they didn't call me to make sure I was still where I said I was. I could have been a murderer. I couldn't believe it really: here I was telling them I was in this country illegally and no one even wanted to make sure I wasn't a criminal.

A month later I was back in London. More basic questions. They took my fingerprints, photos. They asked me why we didn't just say no to Assad, why we didn't stand up to him. They didn't seem to know anything about what was really going on over there. I am a father with three daughters; you can't just say no to a dictator. You would be killed. They asked me why my wife's surname was different to mine. In Syria, women keep their names when they marry, but they made me feel like I was trying to hide something.

And then it was another three months, no contact again, while I waited for my second interview. How can a person live in a new country for months and months with no support and unable to work? I was lucky I had my family who were happy to help, but I wanted to support myself. As a refugee you cannot work, even fully trained doctors cannot work, and we need them here! Officially, you are entitled to a small amount of money each week from the government, but it's nowhere near enough to live on, and every time I phoned up I was told it was 'in process'.

And as I quickly found out, people are very happy to take advantage of the desperation of asylum seekers.

That's when I moved down closer to London and found work in a carwash. I didn't want to work illegally, but months and months of doing nothing is hard. It's hard for someone like me, who has always supported themself, to have to depend so much on others. And it is very difficult mentally, to be in limbo, to be constantly wondering, what's next? What is happening? Has something gone wrong? You can get lost inside your own head. I always try to look for the good in any experience I have, but to be honest there wasn't a lot of good to be found at that time. I was treated badly at the carwash, I was underpaid, I slept in a portacabin. I was there 24 hours a day. People exploit other people in vulnerable situations, but I didn't really have a choice.

But 26 April 2016, six months after I had arrived in the UK, was a good day: my asylum seeker status was finally approved, which meant I was able to work legally. Even better, it meant I could submit my family reunion application and I started to let myself look forward to seeing my wife and daughters again. For some people, it can take a year for their application to be processed, but this time I was very lucky and in just three months, it had been granted.

Reuniting with my family in July 2016 was one of the most incredible moments of my life. It was something we had all been dreaming about, but hadn't wanted to hope for in case it took much longer than we expected, or didn't happen at all. The Home Office then granted us five years leave to remain in the UK, meaning we could live here for five years before applying for indefinite leave to remain. But after one year, you can apply for your UK citizenship. It costs a lot of money and involves a lot of stupid tests to 'prove' your knowledge of life as a British citizen. Questions about its history, its laws and customs. Questions like 'who won an Olympic gold for swimming in the 1970s?'. Questions I'm sure many life-long British citizens would not know the answer to. But at midnight, exactly one year after we received our leave to remain, we sent in our applications for citizenship. We were ready and prepared, we had done all we could. What we weren't prepared for was the waiting that followed.

With my mother passing, my father had somehow been left behind and I knew I had to find a way to bring him over too. The Home Office rejected him as part of my family reunion application, because they said he wasn't family . . . My back and forth with them went on for a long time and ended in me taking them to court. I said I'd sponsor a visa for him, that I didn't need anything from the Home Office, I just wanted him to be with us. And in March 2018 he joined us in the UK, living between my sister's family and mine.

For many people I knew, their citizenship application took a few weeks to be approved, maybe a couple of months. We waited eleven long months with no updates. Waiting, waiting. Is there something wrong with my papers? Are they investigating something? I had a parking ticket, would that mean they'd send me back to Syria? Why does this person have their citizenship after just six weeks and we haven't? Then came the rumours that they'd be changing the citizenship laws soon. And then the Home Secretary revealed plans to send asylum seekers to Rwanda. Would we be among them? Even though we were so far down the process? So much worry, so much uncertainty, so much anxiety. And every time I phoned up, I was told 'it's in process, it's still being processed.'

We were now in 2022, so by this stage I was running a successful restaurant, employing people, my wife ran a catering company, we were paying taxes, my children were in school. What did we do? What more could we do?

And then, in December 2022, we finally received our official British citizenship.

I literally cannot describe what that meant to us. It was a very, very emotional moment for me. I had been dreaming of this moment for years, to belong somewhere fully again. You don't have to have British citizenship in order to be a Londoner, and I don't have any more loyalty to my new city because I am now a legal citizen. For me, I was accepted into this country when the people welcomed me in. When they tried my food and enjoyed it. When they hugged me in the street, followed my story on Instagram, when they told me gently that they were happy I was here. That was when I honestly felt like I was part of something again, when I had a home. I had my own citizenship a long time before it was granted by the Home Office, but we couldn't be deported now. We were safe.

MOUSSAKA

This is a Syrian version, and although it's called moussaka, it's not the one everyone will know. It's vegan, and a classic dish to be eaten during Christian fasting times. In Syria we deep-fry the aubergines, but I've adapted this recipe to be a little healthier, easier and a little less greasy.

TO MAKE

✧ ✧ ✧ ✧ ✧ ✧ ✧ ✧ ✧ ✧ ✧ ✧ ✧ ✧ ✧ ✧ ✧ ✧ ✧ ✧

3 aubergines
3 – 4 tablespoons olive oil
Salt

Using a swivel vegetable peeler, peel off the skin from the aubergines in vertical stripes, so you're left with some skin on; this will give them a little more smoky taste. Now cut them lengthways into slices 2cm thick.

Place the aubergine slices in a single layer over a few baking trays, salt them generously then lay over some kitchen paper to soak up the moisture that will come out of them – this will take about 10 minutes. Replace the damp paper with fresh dry paper to remove as much moisture as you can, patting them all down. This is important as you want your aubergines to be as dry as possible so you won't have a soggy moussaka.

Preheat the oven to 200°C/Fan 180°C/gas 6. Add 2 – 3 tablespoons of olive oil to the now-dry aubergines, rub it all over, then roast in the oven for 15 minutes until golden.

FOR THE SAUCE

✧ ✧ ✧ ✧ ✧ ✧ ✧ ✧ ✧ ✧ ✧ ✧ ✧ ✧ ✧ ✧ ✧ ✧ ✧ ✧

2 tablespoons olive oil
1 teaspoon cumin seeds
5 garlic cloves, very finely sliced
1 tablespoon tomato purée
2 x 400g tins of tomatoes
1 teaspoon ground black pepper
2 long green peppers
  or bell peppers, deseeded
  and finely sliced

Meanwhile, for the sauce, add 2 tablespoons of olive oil to a large saucepan over a medium heat. Add the cumin seeds and toast for a minute, then add the garlic and tomato purée for a few minutes to cook out. Now add the tinned tomatoes and black pepper and simmer for 5 minutes.

Remove the aubergines from the oven and layer them all into an oven dish 30 x 20cm. Pour over the tomato sauce, followed by the sliced green peppers and a little more olive oil. Return to the oven for another 30 minutes. We don't want to cook the peppers through here; they are supposed to still have a little bite, so don't worry if they aren't soft.

TO SERVE

✧ ✧ ✧ ✧ ✧ ✧ ✧ ✧ ✧ ✧ ✧ ✧ ✧ ✧ ✧ ✧ ✧ ✧ ✧ ✧

Small handful of parsley,
  finely chopped
Bulgur wheat
Pickles
Green plate (page 45)

Finish with chopped parsley and serve with bulgur wheat and pickles. This is a dish that is most definitely served with a green plate.

FILO RICE

TO MAKE

✦ ✦ ✦ ✦ ✦ ✦ ✦ ✦ ✦ ✦ ✦ ✦ ✦ ✦ ✦ ✦ ✦ ✦ ✦ ✦

450g diced lamb leg
2 bay leaves
3 cardamom pods
2 cloves
200g long-grain rice
1 teaspoon cumin seeds
2 tablespoons olive oil
Pinch of salt
½ teaspoon ground cardamom
½ teaspoon ground ginger
1 teaspoon baharat (page 32)
200g frozen peas
40g pine nuts, toasted
40g cashew nuts, toasted
  and roughly chopped
½ teaspoon ground black pepper
1 x 270g packet of filo pastry
4 tablespoons melted ghee

Add the lamb to a large pot with enough water to cover (about 1 litre) and bring to the boil over a high heat. Once it starts to boil, you'll see a foamy layer rise to the surface; remove this with a spoon. Once all the foam has been removed, add the bay leaves, cardamom pods and cloves and turn down to a simmer. Cover with a lid and cook for 45–60 minutes until soft. Drain the lamb, keeping the cooking water.

Meanwhile, wash the rice until the water runs clear, soak in a bowl of cold water for 30 minutes, then drain.

In a pan over a medium-high heat, toast the cumin seeds in the olive oil for a minute, then add the drained rice, salt and ground spices to the pan and cover half with reserved lamb cooking water and half water; the liquid should come about 1cm above the rice. Cover and increase the heat to a boil, then immediately turn down to a very low simmer for 15 minutes. Take off the heat and leave for 5 minutes. Separate the rice with a fork and transfer to a tray to cool evenly.

Once everything is cooled, mix together the lamb, rice, peas, nuts and black pepper. Set aside.

Unroll your filo pastry and cover with a tea towel (this is important as you don't want the filo pastry to dry out).

Preheat the oven to 200°C/Fan 180°C/gas 6. Brush some melted ghee over into a low-sided baking tray, to grease it.

Take one sheet of filo and fold in half and then in half again, so you have 4 layers. Press the filo into a ramekin dish so it moulds into the shape, but make sure you have an overhang to be able to fold over the top of the filling later. Fill the filo with rice and lamb mixture and fold the filo over the mixture to close it up.

Working quickly, put a hand over the closed filo and ramekin and flip over onto the ghee-lined tray, so you have an upside-down parcel. Brush generously with ghee and repeat with the remaining rice and filo to make 5 more.

Bake for 30–35 minutes until the filo is golden all over.

TO SERVE

✦ ✦ ✦ ✦ ✦ ✦ ✦ ✦ ✦ ✦ ✦ ✦ ✦ ✦ ✦ ✦ ✦ ✦ ✦ ✦

Laban bikhiar (page 97)
Green salad

Remove from the oven and serve with laban bikhiar or green salad.

FWL MUDAMIS

Fava beans

You can find canned fava beans in most supermarkets.

FOR THE GREEN PASTE

✧ ✧ ✧ ✧ ✧ ✧ ✧ ✧ ✧ ✧ ✧ ✧ ✧ ✧ ✧ ✧ ✧ ✧

3 garlic cloves
1 green chilli
Bunch of parsley, stalks only
  (save the leaves for serving)
Juice of 2 lemons
1 teaspoon ground cumin
½ teaspoon salt
2 tablespoons olive oil

Make the green paste by adding all the ingredients to a food processor and blitzing briefly, so it's still a little chunky.

TO MAKE

✧ ✧ ✧ ✧ ✧ ✧ ✧ ✧ ✧ ✧ ✧ ✧ ✧ ✧ ✧ ✧ ✧ ✧

200g dried broad beans/whole
  fava beans (you can use canned,
  or canned chickpeas work
  well instead)
1.5 litres water
½ teaspoon bicarbonate of soda
Small bunch of parsley, leaves only
Small bunch of mint, leaves only
1 beef tomato or 3 vine tomatoes,
  cut into 1cm cubes
½ red onion, finely diced
2 tablespoons extra virgin olive oil
Salt and ground black pepper

Soak the dried beans overnight in plenty of water. Drain and place in a pan with the measured water. Add the bicarb, bring to the boil then simmer for 90 minutes, or until softened.

Drain the beans (if using canned, warm the beans through first) into a bowl and add the green sauce along with the herb leaves, tomato, onion and extra virgin olive oil. Stir together to combine.

TO SERVE

✧ ✧ ✧ ✧ ✧ ✧ ✧ ✧ ✧ ✧ ✧ ✧ ✧ ✧ ✧ ✧ ✧ ✧

Hummus (page 68)
Flatbread
Chilli peppers
Laban bikhiar (page 97)

I love this served with hummus, flatbread and chilli, but it's also delicious with laban bikhiar.

BARGHIL BIALKUSA

Bulgur wheat with courgette

TO MAKE

❖ ❖ ❖ ❖ ❖ ❖ ❖ ❖ ❖ ❖ ❖ ❖ ❖ ❖ ❖ ❖ ❖ ❖

100ml extra virgin olive oil
1 teaspoon cumin seeds
2 red onions, finely chopped
½ teaspoon ground cumin
1 teaspoon baharat (page 32)
Pinch of salt
½ teaspoon freshly ground
   black pepper
4 courgettes, cut into 2cm chunks
Small bunch of dill, chopped
Small bunch of coriander, chopped
5 garlic cloves, crushed to a paste
300g coarse bulgur wheat

Add half the oil to a saucepan over a medium heat, then add the cumin seeds and toast for a minute. Add the chopped onions with the ground cumin, baharat, salt and pepper, then stir to coat in the oil. Cook for 5–6 minutes until soft.

Add the courgettes to the pan with the onions and spices. Stir and cook for a further 5–6 minutes until the courgettes are slightly softened.

Stir in the chopped dill, coriander and crushed garlic and mix it all together so everything is coated. Now add the bulgur wheat and the remaining oil. Add in enough water to cover the bulgur and courgettes (about 1cm above everything), bring to the boil then lower the heat to its lowest for 5–6 minutes. Take off the heat and allow it to sit, covered with a lid, for 2 minutes. When you lift the lid the bulgur will be perfectly cooked, so just break up the grains with a fork.

TO SERVE

❖ ❖ ❖ ❖ ❖ ❖ ❖ ❖ ❖ ❖ ❖ ❖ ❖ ❖ ❖ ❖ ❖

Laban bikhiar (page 97)
Green salad

Serve with laban bikhiar and a green salad.

FIVE

DESSERTS

DESSERTS

BAKLAWA

This recipe won't work with English filo pastry, as it's too thick; you need to get the proper filo for baklawa that you'll find in Middle Eastern shops.

The trick to good baklawa is to be quick and careful. Get everything ready around you before you start, including a large, clean tea towel to keep the filo from drying out while you're making it. This is a pistachio and walnut version, but you can use any nuts you like. I like to use a mix.

TO MAKE

❖ ❖ ❖ ❖ ❖ ❖ ❖ ❖ ❖ ❖ ❖ ❖ ❖ ❖ ❖ ❖

150g shelled pistachios
150g walnuts
1 teaspoon sugar
1 teaspoon orange blossom water
1 teaspoon water
100g good-quality ghee
470 – 500g Turkish, extra-thin
   filo pastry

Preheat the oven to 170°C/Fan 150°C/gas 3½.

Start by toasting the nuts in a large baking tin in a single layer in the oven for 5 minutes. Remove and allow to cool. Add the sugar, orange blossom water and water, then crush the nuts either using a pestle and mortar or a blender. Be careful if using a blender as you want a very chunky texture, not a fine crumb. The water and sugar should make your nuts delicious and sticky.

Melt the ghee in a pan over a low heat and set aside to stay warm. Brush a baking tin (with sides), 35 x 25cm, with a little ghee.

Unroll the filo it so it's flat on the work surface, then lay the prepared baking tin on top of the filo and cut around the edge, so your filo is the exact same size. Remove the excess edges (use in another recipe), then place the cut filo in a clean tea towel to keep it from drying out (you should have at 24 layers of filo).

Place half the filo layers in the greased tin, then sprinkle with all the nuts. Spread them out into an even layer and pat them down a little. Now top with the other half of the filo layers, and, with the back of a spoon, tuck in the edges of the filo, so that they curl in neatly down the sides of the tin. Working quickly so the filo doesn't dry out, slice your baklawa into diamonds. I prefer them small, and make 40, but you can choose any size you like here.

If your ghee has cooled, reheat it again to melt, pour it over everything, then bake in the oven for 35 – 40 minutes until golden on top.

FOR THE SYRUP

❖ ❖ ❖ ❖ ❖ ❖ ❖ ❖ ❖ ❖ ❖ ❖ ❖ ❖ ❖ ❖ ❖ ❖

500g caster sugar
400ml water
1 slice of lemon
3 cardamom pods
1 cinnamon stick
1 teaspoon orange blossom water

While it's baking, make your syrup. Put the sugar and water in a heavy-based saucepan over a medium heat and stir well until the sugar has dissolved. Add the lemon slice, cardamom and cinnamon, then bring to the boil. Turn down to a gentle simmer for 5 minutes, then take off the heat and stir in the orange blossom water. Remove the cardamom and cinnamon.

Remove the baklawa from the oven then drain any excess ghee from the bottom. I do this by placing a clean tray on top of the baked baklawa and tipping it carefully so the ghee pours out from the bottom corner into a bowl (you can use this ghee for your next baklawa).

Now pour over your hot sugar syrup, one ladleful at a time as you might not use it all. It's important that it's hot here; it should sizzle a bit when it's poured over. Continue to spoon over the syrup until it comes halfway up the baklawa. Allow to sit for a minute then drain off the excess syrup, the same way you did the ghee.

Serve hot or allow to cool then cover with foil.

ROLLED BAKLAWA

This is a variation on traditional baklawa.

Pictured overleaf.

TO MAKE

✦ ✦ ✦ ✦ ✦ ✦ ✦ ✦ ✦ ✦ ✦ ✦ ✦ ✦ ✦ ✦ ✦ ✦ ✦ ✦

150g shelled pistachios
150g walnuts
1 teaspoon sugar
1 teaspoon orange blossom water
1 teaspoon water
150g good-quality ghee, melted
270g Turkish, extra-thin
  filo pastry
1 quantity syrup (see opposite)

Preheat the oven to 170°C/Fan 150°C/gas 3½.

Follow the steps as for the main baklawa recipe to toast and grind the nuts with the sugar and orange blossom water and water, and grease the baking tin with melted ghee.

Take 2 sheets of filo and place them one on top of the other lengthways in front of you. Scatter a heaped tablespoon of nuts over the filo sheet, then place a long skewer vertically in the middle of the filo sheet. Fold the sheet over, then roll it up, using the skewer to help. Lift the roll into the tray and then push the nut-filled filo off the skewer so it ruffles in the tin. Tuck it into the ends of the tin.

Repeat with all the filo and nuts until the tin is filled with the ruffled rolls.

Working quickly so the filo doesn't dry out, slice each rolled length into 6–8 pieces. I prefer them this smaller size, but you can choose any size you like here.

Pour the melted ghee over everything then bake in the oven for 35–40 minutes until golden on top.

While they are baking, make your sugar syrup following the instructions opposite.

Remove the baklawa from the oven then drain any excess ghee from the bottom (see opposite). Pour over your hot sugar syrup (see opposite).

Serve hot or allow to cool, then cover with foil.

ANGELS

MY WHOLE LIFE, I have been surrounded by angels. Despite everything I have been through, everything I have seen, I know I am one of the lucky ones. I've always felt as though when I've needed help the most, someone has been there for me. And that is why I always try to be there for the people around me too.

I struggled so much on my journey from Syria. It was the hardest thing I've ever done in my life. Crossing from Turkey in the boat, landing on the Greek coast, I was completely shattered from the inside. We were cold, exhausted, afraid of what came next, wearing our orange life jackets and holding onto our few possessions, the only things left that told anything about who we really were. But then we looked up and saw an older lady waving and shouting down to us from the small cliff above the beach 'You are safe now, don't be scared!' And in that moment, I was so relieved. When I looked at her face, she looked so happy. Happier than I felt right then, even though I was in Europe, finally. She was jumping around all over the place wanting to help everyone, to reach us, to let us know we'd be OK now. We took photos together, but I was so overwhelmed, I wasn't able to thank her properly. And then just as she had arrived, she disappeared. It took a few hours for us all to figure out what was going to happen next and in that time I spoke to a volunteer doctor, helping translate for a pregnant woman who had been on our boat. I asked about the woman who had been waving to us and was told she was Norwegian, that she'd used her holiday from work to help refugees as they arrived in Greece. She was actually on her way back to the airport now, back to Norway, but had seen our boat coming in and wanted to come down to greet us first. I am so frustrated that I don't know her name. I want to thank her so much for making us feel welcome, for making us feel human again.

⊹

ON THE TRAIN from Stuttgart, I had no idea what I was going to do when I arrived in Paris. I don't speak French and I had never been there before, I had no idea what to expect or where to go. I looked up and down the train carriage, trying to work out a plan, when I saw a man, minding his own business, reading the Quran in Arabic. I went over to him and explained my situation: that I had been travelling through illegally, I didn't know where I was going to in Paris, and I was so, so tired. I needed a mattress and a shower, and that I could pay. I asked if he knew of anywhere I'd be safe.

He asked me what kind of hotel I needed. And I replied the cheapest one! Anything would do. He said he knew someone who worked in a hotel near Gard de Nord, and that he'd come with me to help me find the hotel, to check I was OK. It was a stop beyond his journey, but he came with me anyway, and when we got to the reception he started speaking in French with his friend. They told me to go up to the room to see if I liked it and if I did, I could stay in it, I'd be safe. All I needed was a passport. I said I didn't need to go up, that I was sure it was perfect, but they insisted and I went up to drop off my bag. I was gone for no more than five minutes, but when I came back down the man on reception said my room had been paid for two nights by the man from the train, and also my dinner that evening. He had already left, so I couldn't thank him. I found out his name was Achmed and he was Algerian-French, but the hotelier didn't have his contact details.

You see how lucky I am? I only asked for an address of a hotel, but instead he insisted he came all the way with me, to ensure that I was safe inside the hotel. I will always be grateful to Achmed for helping a stranger who was in need.

✢

WHEN I ARRIVED IN CALAIS, I knew immediately that I couldn't stay in The Jungle. The local gendarme was trying to keep everyone in the camp so they could keep control over them, but to me it felt lawless. I didn't even go inside. When I arrived in the city it was late at night. I didn't know anyone. I was a refugee with a Syrian passport, I was too afraid to go to a hotel. Along the way you kept hearing stories of police beating people, and I was emotionally and mentally prepared to be scared. I was cold and alone and didn't know what to do. And then I saw some Sudanese people walking past and asked them if they knew where I could stay. They asked me if I was Syrian and then pointed me towards a church where they said some other Syrians were sleeping. The church was in a square, but when I got there, I couldn't see any Syrians, just a very blonde woman sitting on top of some mattresses. I introduced myself and started to explain my situation, and for ten minutes she interrogated me, asking more questions, checking out my story. She then told me that she was keeping the mattresses safe while the Syrian men who were camping here tried to cross The Channel. They'd be able to explain to me how it all worked, if they came back, if their attempt was unsuccessful. In the meantime I could stay, and if they returned I could tell them Frederike said I could stay. She left me on the church steps, but 15 minutes later returned with a jacket, a blanket, a pillow, some painkillers and some muscle-relaxing cream because my back was in a lot of pain. And also, hot tea and dinner. You can't imagine how I felt!

Every single morning Frederike would go for a jog, running past the church. And every morning – she didn't miss one day for the 64 days I was there – she'd put a fresh pot of tea down for us with a note next to it written on

a napkin that said 'Have a great morning' with a smiley face, or 'have a great day'.
Always with a smiley face. She never forgot the tea and she never forgot the note.
We are still in touch today, in fact we're great friends. She's stayed with my family,
and we've been to visit hers. She was there when we opened the restaurant.

✤

THEN THERE WERE TWO FRENCH WOMEN who were driving through Calais on
their way back to Paris after a holiday in the UK. They wanted to find out more about
the situation and found us at our church. We were cooking at the time. They asked
if they could talk to us. 'Of course! But first try our food!' 'Before I try your food, can
I take your photo?' 'Yes!' They were so friendly, so interested in trying to understand
the situation in Syria, the situation in Calais, what it meant to be here. We cooked
mujadama and they loved it, the spices, the flavours. We swapped numbers, and then
they left. When the gendarme kicked us off the church steps, she called me and asked
if we were OK, where we'd be going next. She said it was all over the French news that
they were taking everyone to The Jungle. I told her I didn't feel safe in Calais anymore
and that we were heading to Paris, back to the hotel I'd stayed in before. 'No,' she said.
She'd meet me from my train and we could stay with her in her apartment. They
emptied a room in their apartment and three of us, me and two friends, stayed there
for 13 days. It was from her apartment that I left to get the Eurostar to London.

✤

WHEN MY FAMILY were able to join me in the UK, when the family reunion application
had been approved, I could barely afford to live by myself, let alone support them.
I had got them out of Syria to Lebanon, and the charity Choose Love helped with their
plane tickets from Beirut to the UK. That was the beginning of a long relationship
with that charity and its founder, Josie, who I work with a lot today. My family and
I moved to High Wycombe, and it was through the local community that I met Toni
(who introduced me to Cook For Syria, see page 10) and her friend Stephanie, both
of them true angels. Toni and Stephanie helped me find a house to rent for my family
and taught me about the system so I could get my children registered in school. The
house was a little bit depressing inside, dirty, in need of lots of repairs. But it was big
enough and honestly, it was perfect; it was our first family home together where we
would be safe. After I'd paid the first month's rent, Stephanie told us to come back the
next day at noon, and when we arrived, it was almost a different house. They'd found
furniture for the rooms, they'd made up the girls' bedroom, they'd cleaned it for us
– they'd made it feel like a home. I remember walking into the house and Stephanie
was lying on the floor, sweeping under the fridge! She was not a young woman! I can't
describe how welcome this made us, how happy we were, how supported we felt as we
started our new life. We are still close with Toni and Stephanie today, even though
we now live in Ickenham. My children see Stephanie as a grandmother. They have
a very special and beautiful relationship together and it's wonderful to see.

THERE HAVE BEEN so many people like the lady from Norway, like Achmed, like Frederike, like Toni and Stephanie; hundreds of angels all along the way on this journey of mine. In Calais, someone gave us a big comfy chair to sit on on the steps of the church, and a British Pakistani gave us the hob to cook on and a pot and a knife – he's a very good friend of mine now. These small things, they don't seem much, but they changed our lives. A Lebanese British man, another great friend now, stopped and asked me 'Are you Syrian? I'm coming back to Calais next week – I hope you make it across in that time – but tell me what you miss the most and I can bring it from the UK.' 'Syrian coffee!' I said, 'I miss Syrian coffee and Syrian bread!' He didn't even wait a week, he came back the next day with a huge van full of cans of chickpeas and fava beans, coffee, bread, vegetables, nuts, chocolate bars and crisps. One of the neighbours near the church left out 12 electrical sockets next to his door every day so we could recharge our mobiles and not spend 5 euros to sit in a local cafe. At 1pm one of us would put all the mobile phones in and come back at 6pm to collect them. Every single day. Other neighbours used to come to us and translate the newspaper for us if there was anything about the refugees in Calais.

Although most of the angels in my life have been strangers, showing kindness to others without even knowing their situation, I am so, so lucky to have angels within my own family too. When we were still in Syria, moving around for our safety, my brother Mohammad took us into his home and helped us out financially when my businesses were destroyed. My sister Rania and brother-in-law Thabet too: they left Syria before we did, but let us stay in their house in Damascus. And when I came to the UK, they opened up their home to me again in Doncaster. Thabet is someone you can depend on. He's almost like a mythical personality, doing good, looking for ways he can support people all the time. I can't thank them all enough for being there when we needed them.

I have so many people to thank for getting me to where I am, so many angels I've met, who arrived when I was at my lowest. Despite the horrors I've seen in the world, that we hear about every day on the news, I know that there is also so much goodness out there. I believe that when you have love in your heart, you will find it in other people's faces. Build love in your heart and you will see it in others around you too.

DATE AND TAHINI SWEET DIP

SERVES 2–4

This is so delicious, and actually makes the best breakfast! You can make as much as you want and put it in a jar to have every morning or as an evening treat.

TO MAKE

❖ ❖ ❖ ❖ ❖ ❖ ❖ ❖ ❖ ❖ ❖ ❖ ❖ ❖ ❖ ❖

2 tablespoons date molasses
2 tablespoons tahini
50g toasted sesame seeds

Mix the ingredients together in a small bowl and serve with flatbreads or toast.

MAHALAYA

Mastic gum is a natural tree sap that acts like a gelatine, but with flavour. You can find it online and I really recommend getting hold of it.

TO MAKE

❖ ❖ ❖ ❖ ❖ ❖ ❖ ❖ ❖ ❖ ❖ ❖ ❖ ❖ ❖ ❖ ❖

1 litre whole milk
65g cornflour
100g caster sugar
2 bay leaves
2 pieces of mastic gum
150ml double cream
100g condensed milk
2 teaspoons orange
  blossom water

Pour the milk into a bowl, add the cornflour and 90g of the sugar, then whisk well until the sugar has dissolved.

Now pour the mixture into a large saucepan over a medium-high heat with the bay leaves. Bring to the boil, then turn down to low and simmer for a few minutes until slightly thickened.

Using a pestle and mortar, crush the mastic gum and remaining 10g sugar together until very, very fine (like table salt).

Add the mastic a little at a time to the milk, still over the heat (it's very important it's still hot), whisking as you go, then whisk in the cream followed by the condensed milk and orange blossom water. Take off the heat and pour into ramekins or glasses.

Allow to cool for 1 hour, then set in the fridge for 6 hours, or ideally overnight.

TO SERVE

❖ ❖ ❖ ❖ ❖ ❖ ❖ ❖ ❖ ❖ ❖ ❖ ❖ ❖ ❖ ❖ ❖

150ml double cream,
  lightly whipped
Glacé cherries
Shelled pistachios
Fresh mint
Strawberries or any berries
  in season
Desiccated coconut

Serve decorated with lightly whipped cream, glacé cherries and pistachios, fresh mint, fruit or desiccated coconut, or any combination.

TAMRIAH

Dates with biscuits

It's really important to taste your dates here. Sometimes they come from Jordan and they aren't as sweet as the ones from Iraq or Saudi Arabia.

TO MAKE

✧ ✧ ✧ ✧ ✧ ✧ ✧ ✧ ✧ ✧ ✧ ✧ ✧ ✧ ✧ ✧ ✧

100g almonds, cashews and
  pistachios (all or just one
  of these, whichever you like)
50g walnuts
2 tablespoons ghee
650g medjool dates, pitted and
  roughly chopped
½ teaspoon ground cardamom
½ teaspoon ground cinnamon
2 teaspoons orange blossom water
150g plain Rich Tea
  or similar biscuits

Preheat the oven to 180°C/Fan 160°C/gas 4.

Toast your nuts on a large baking tray for 5 minutes until lightly golden, then set aside to cool. Once cool, roughly chop.

Melt the ghee in a medium saucepan over a low heat. Add the chopped dates and stir for a few minutes until the dates have softened into the ghee. Now add the cardamom, cinnamon and orange blossom water. Stir it all together so it creates a paste – I put on a plastic glove and mash it together with my hand, but you can just get a potato masher or something similar to mix it to a paste.

In a bowl, crush the biscuits with your hands into a rough crumble; it's good to have some larger chunks for bite, so don't go too fine. Add to the pan with the date paste.

Line a 20cm square baking tray with baking paper then spoon in your chunky date mixture. Even out the mixture to 1cm thick, sprinkle the nuts evenly over the top, then press them into the dates. Set in the fridge for 1 hour, then slice into however many pieces you want.

These will keep for a week in a container out of direct sunlight.

BIRD'S NEST

FOR THE NEST

❖ ❖ ❖ ❖ ❖ ❖ ❖ ❖ ❖ ❖ ❖ ❖ ❖ ❖ ❖ ❖ ❖ ❖

40g shelled pistachios
300g kataifi pastry

Soak the pistachios in water for 30 minutes, then drain.

Cover the kataifi with a damp tea towel so it doesn't dry out as you work. Take a finely twisted 30cm length of pastry and wrap it in a circular motion around two fingers into a nest shape. Transfer to a baking tray, then repeat with the rest of the pastry.

Drain the pistachios and gently press 4 or 5 into the middle of each nest. Cover the nests with a layer of baking paper, then put another baking tray on top and put a heavy weight (1kg) on top of the paper. Leave at room temperature for 1 hour, then remove the weight, tray and baking paper and leave for another hour to dry out.

FOR THE SYRUP

❖ ❖ ❖ ❖ ❖ ❖ ❖ ❖ ❖ ❖ ❖ ❖ ❖ ❖ ❖ ❖ ❖ ❖

400g sugar
500ml water
2 tablespoons lemon juice

Meanwhile, for the syrup, dissolve the sugar in the water in a pan over a medium heat, bring to the boil and bubble for 15–20 minutes or until reduced and lightly syrupy. Stir in the lemon juice and boil for a further minute. Remove from the heat and set aside.

TO ASSEMBLE

❖ ❖ ❖ ❖ ❖ ❖ ❖ ❖ ❖ ❖ ❖ ❖ ❖ ❖ ❖ ❖ ❖ ❖

375g butter, melted

Preheat the oven to 220°C/Fan 200°C/gas 7.

Pour the butter over and around the nests, so that they're sitting in a layer of melted butter. Cook for 20–25 minutes until golden brown, turning the tray from time to time to make sure the nests are evenly coloured. Leave to cool for 10 minutes, then transfer to a clean baking tray and pour over the syrup. Leave to cool completely in the syrup, then serve.

BESBUSI

FOR THE SPONGE

✣ ✣ ✣ ✣ ✣ ✣ ✣ ✣ ✣ ✣ ✣ ✣ ✣ ✣ ✣ ✣ ✣

300g medium semolina
150g desiccated coconut
½ teaspoon ground cardamom
50g milk powder
1½ teaspoons baking powder
Pinch of salt
3 eggs
150g sugar
1½ teaspoons vanilla paste
200g vegetable oil
300g yogurt
Zest of 1 lemon
2 tablespoons tahini
Handful of skinned almonds

Preheat the oven to 180°C/Fan 160°C/gas 4.

In a mixing bowl, add the semolina, desiccated coconut, cardamom, milk powder, baking powder and salt and mix to combine.

In another bowl, whisk the eggs, sugar, vanilla, vegetable oil, yogurt and lemon zest together until smooth, then add this to the dry ingredients, mixing until you have a smooth batter.

Grease a 30 x 40 cm baking tin with 1 tablespoon of tahini then pour in the batter. Smooth out the top with the back of a spoon then tap on a surface to remove any air. Scatter over or arrange the almonds and place on the middle shelf of the oven for 30 minutes.

FOR THE SUGAR SYRUP

✣ ✣ ✣ ✣ ✣ ✣ ✣ ✣ ✣ ✣ ✣ ✣ ✣ ✣ ✣ ✣ ✣

100g water
100g sugar
1 slice of lemon
1½ tablespoons ghee

While the cake is in the oven, add the water and sugar to a small saucepan and slowly bring to the boil. Once boiling, turn down to a simmer for 3 minutes then add in the slice of lemon.

Melt the ghee in the sugar syrup and place over a very low heat to keep warm until the cake is ready.

TO FINISH

✣ ✣ ✣ ✣ ✣ ✣ ✣ ✣ ✣ ✣ ✣ ✣ ✣ ✣ ✣ ✣ ✣

Remove the cake from the oven, and immediately pour over two-thirds of the warm syrup. Set the rest of the syrup aside.

Slice into 24 squares then pour over the remaining syrup.

Leave to cool in the tin for 30 minutes and serve warm or cold. Store in an airtight container in a cool dark place for 4 – 5 days.

IBIZA KONAFA

I created this when I was catering in Ibiza in 2018 and 2019 in Pikes hotel, where I went to cook for the charity Choose Love.

FOR THE FILLING

❖ ❖ ❖ ❖ ❖ ❖ ❖ ❖ ❖ ❖ ❖ ❖ ❖ ❖ ❖ ❖

100g mixed nuts (use whatever you have – I like cashews, walnuts and pistachios)
1 quantity sugar syrup (page 222) or agave syrup
½ teaspoon ground cardamom
3 tablespoons double cream

Preheat the oven to 200°C/Fan 180°C/gas 6. Grease a 12-hole muffin tin with a little ghee.

Tip the nuts onto a baking tray and toast in the oven for 5 minutes, then remove and allow to cool before blitzing in a food processor with 2 tablespoons of the sugar syrup and the ground cardamom until you have a rough, sticky crumb. Now add the cream and blitz once more until combined.

FOR THE PASTRY

❖ ❖ ❖ ❖ ❖ ❖ ❖ ❖ ❖ ❖ ❖ ❖ ❖ ❖ ❖ ❖

200g konafa pastry
100g ghee, plus extra for greasing
¼ tsp ground cardamom
Generous pinch of saffron strands

Crush the konafa pastry into fine pieces in a bowl. Melt the ghee with the cardamom and saffron, then pour over the crushed konafa. Mix with your hands until evenly coated.

Spoon 1 generous tablespoon of the konafa into each muffin hole, using up half the mixture. Press the konafa down with your fingers so it's evenly compressed, then add a tablespoon of the creamy nut filling to each, or until you have used it all up and distributed it evenly. Add the remaining konafa to the tops, pressing it in.

Bake in the oven for 25 minutes until lightly golden and starting to crisp. Meanwhile, heat up the remaining sugar syrup.

Remove the konafa from the oven and immediately pour 1 tablespoon of the hot sugar syrup over each konafa.

Get a large baking tray similar in size to the muffin tin, and carefully and quickly flip the hot tray over so the konafa tip out. Allow to cool slightly then serve warm, or cold.

WHY SYRIANS FEEL
LEFT BEHIND

RIGHT NOW, EVERYONE I KNOW is trying to escape from Syria. The situation there has never been more desperate. But sometimes I feel as though the world has forgotten Syria, that they've moved on, left us behind. Assad's rule is as harsh as ever, worse than before, but even now they call Hafez al-Assad, Bashar's father, 'the immortal commander'. Ten hours a day, news cycles on Syrian TV talk about Assad's glory. It just keeps going. One day, surely, it must end, but I can't imagine when or how. I hope I will be alive to see it happen, for my daughters.

I think for many people outside of Syria, especially in Western and European countries, Syria feels too far away, both geographically and in terms of our lifestyle. But we were no different to you. Our lives were the same: we worked, our children went to school, our cities were busy and modern, we enjoyed our social lives, we ran our own businesses, we had all the same dreams for ourselves and our families.

There may not be as many rocket bombs falling each night now, but there is no gas, no electricity, no money left to run the infrastructure to support normal life. In Damascus you get power for a couple of hours each day, but in other cities, in rural areas, it might be an hour a couple of times a week if you're lucky. People work twelve hours a day, but don't have enough to buy the basics. Without the help of friends and family outside of Syria, you cannot get by. But it's so risky to receive that help, the regime would view it as supporting ISIS or bringing down Syria from the inside. It's a dark, dangerous time, with people dying in jails, or disappearing with no hope of being found.

People call it a civil war, but it's not our war anymore. It's a complex battlefield playing out between other nations, while ordinary Syrians can only sit by and watch, powerless. Russia and Iran have launched attacks in support of Assad; ISIS and al-Qaeda have taken advantage of the chaos and taken over vast areas of the country; the USA has conducted air strikes on the Islamic State; Turkey launched its own invasion driving out Kurdish-rules areas; Israel is bombing Hezbollah in Syria every single week. And there are many, many smaller, local rebellion groups, fighting to gain their own slice of power. It's a mess. A mess that has resulted in the death of hundreds of thousands and six million people fleeing the country. When I was in Syria, I was the luckiest one of my neighbours as I lost only businesses, not a member of my family, unlike most of them.

So I am shocked when people don't know where Syria is, when they ask how things are now. Honestly, it makes me angry to see the response to the situation in Ukraine, compared with how the world reacted to what happened in Syria. It feels like there are two classes of refugees: and the difference is to do with the colour of our skin. I feel Syrians – and Iranians, and the Sudanese, and so many others – have been failed by governments around the world. We feel betrayed. Hundreds of red lines have been given to Assad, and all of them were crossed, with no repercussions. There are so many good people in the world, I can't tell you how warm the hearts of the UK people are. But their governments are not representing their people. People ask me why we have refugees from Syria here. They don't know it's because their governments didn't do anything to step in and help, they took no action.

Why was it OK for Russia to host the World Cup in 2018 when it was killing people in Syria, but it wasn't acceptable for Russia to compete in the 2022 Olympics because of their attack on Ukraine? I can give you a direct number to the Home Office if you are a Ukrainian refugee, but if you are from any other nation, there is a recorded message to say they can't do anything because they are overwhelmed with assisting Ukrainians. We are all the same, we are all just people, we need to reach out to each other, to listen to each other's stories, to learn from each other.

I have been made to feel so welcome by the people I've met all along my journey. It has rebuilt my faith in humanity, in the innate goodness of people all over the world. But I don't feel like our governments, our leaders, the media are on our side. They are part of the problem, not the solution. There are so many people who are trying so hard to be positive against the whole world, and we need to join together, not make more divisions.

KONAFA NABLESEH

FOR THE SUGAR SYRUP

❖ ❖ ❖ ❖ ❖ ❖ ❖ ❖ ❖ ❖ ❖ ❖ ❖ ❖ ❖ ❖ ❖

100ml water
100g caster sugar
1 slice of lemon

Start with the sugar syrup. Add the water and sugar to a small saucepan and slowly bring to the boil. Once boiling, turn down to a simmer for about 5 minutes then add in the slice of lemon and reduce the heat to the lowest setting while you get everything else ready.

FOR THE KONAFA

❖ ❖ ❖ ❖ ❖ ❖ ❖ ❖ ❖ ❖ ❖ ❖ ❖ ❖ ❖ ❖ ❖

200g tresse cheese or any kind of very salty, hard cheese (akawi)
100g ghee, plus extra for greasing
Few drops of yellow food colouring (optional)
200g konafa pastry, chopped into small pieces
75g mozzarella, grated
Chopped pistachios, to serve

Grate the hard cheese and put it in a bowl of cold water. Then pour out the water and refill again. Repeat this 4 times to get rid of as much salt in the cheese as possible. Drain and put it on a clean, dry tea towel to get as much moisture out as possible.

Melt the ghee in a small saucepan or in the microwave, then add the yellow colouring, if using. Add the konafa pastry to a bowl with the melted ghee and mix really well so it's all evenly coated.

Brush a 30cm non-stick frying pan with a little more ghee, then add the konafa pastry and press it down firmly into the pan. Now add the grated cheeses to the middle of the pastry, leaving a 1.5cm border around the edge.

Place over a medium-low heat, off-centre so the flame or heat sits on the edges and not in the centre. We want to crisp up the bottom very lightly but also melt the cheese on top, so we have to work slowly and carefully. Stand at the hob for about 10 minutes, turning the pan every few seconds so the heat is evenly distributed underneath, until you can see the edges turning golden and the cheese is melted on top.

Get your serving plate, one that is larger than the pan. Put the plate on top of the pan and carefully and confidently flip over so the pastry is face up.

Turn the heat up on the syrup for a minute then, while hot, spoon over a few ladlefuls. You won't need all the syrup, so don't overdo it. Finish with chopped pistachios and serve immediately, while it's hot.

EAWAAMA

Donuts in date molasses

This makes a lot, so feel free to halve the recipe.

TO MAKE

❖ ❖ ❖ ❖ ❖ ❖ ❖ ❖ ❖ ❖ ❖ ❖ ❖ ❖ ❖ ❖ ❖ ❖

350ml lukewarm water
7g fast-action dried yeast
½ teaspoon ground cardamom
Pinch of rock or sea salt
Pinch of saffron strands
400g plain flour
1 tablespoon cornflour
2 tablespoons agave syrup
½ teaspoon vanilla extract
1.5 litres vegetable oil, plus extra
   for shaping
Date molasses, to serve

Mix the lukewarm water and yeast together in a jug then set aside for 10 minutes to bubble up.

Using a pestle and mortar, grind the cardamom, salt and saffron.

Sift the flour, cornflour and cardamom mixture into a stand mixer with the dough hook attached. Mix for a few seconds to combine, then slowly pour the yeast and water mix with the mixer running, until evenly combined and there are no flour pockets left. Turn up to full speed for 5 minutes until the dough is slightly stretchy but still quite wet. Remove the bowl from the mixer, put a tea towel or clingfilm over the bowl and set aside to rise for an hour, or until doubled in size.

Pour the vegetable oil into a deep, heavy-based pan and place over a medium-high heat until it reaches 170°C (if you don't have a thermometer, check by getting a little bit of dough and adding it to the oil; if it bubbles and rises to the top, you're ready to go).

Once the dough has risen, wet your hands and mix it gently. Place a small bowl of cold vegetable oil next to the hob, for shaping the donuts.

Get the bowl of dough and a teaspoon, then with your hands grab a handful of the dough and squeeze your hand tightly, until the dough pops out at the top of your fist. Then dip the teaspoon into the cold oil (to prevent the dough from sticking) and scoop the dough that's formed in your hand into it, then drop it into the hot oil. Repeat, dipping the spoon in the cold oil every so often to prevent sticking.

Working in batches, deep-fry for 4–5 minutes until lightly golden, pushing the donuts down in to the oil with a long-handled slotted spoon so they all cook evenly. Remove from the oil using the slotted spoon and transfer to a colander set over a bowl to catch the excess oil. Allow to cool for 10–20 minutes.

We are now going to re-fry them, to give them their distinctive crunchy outer layer. Reheat the oil, but this time to 180°C. Once hot (again, you can test this by adding some leftover dough to the oil, and if it bubbles and floats faster than last time, you're ready).

In batches, re-fry the donuts for a further 3 minutes until golden. Remove from the oil onto kitchen paper, then serve hot, with a generous drizzle of date molasses.

SIX

DRINKS

QAWAH

Coffee

In Syria, we have a mixture of 75%
medium roast and 25% dark roast
in our coffee. We do this ourselves,
but you can buy this mix already made
in shops.

Pictured left.

SERVES 2

2½ espresso cups of water
2 teaspoons ground coffee (Turkish fine grind)

Pour the water into a Turkish coffee pot and place
over a medium-high heat. When the water starts
to boil, take it off the heat. Give it a few seconds then
add the ground coffee. Put it back over the heat until
it's boiling again, then take it off to stir. Continue
to put it back on and off the heat in this way (this is
so it doesn't boil too fast and burn the coffee).

Serve immediately.

TAMARIND JUICE

SERVES 4

1 quantity of tamarind sauce (page 130)
150ml agave syrup or 100g caster sugar
1 teaspoon orange blossom water
1 litre water
1 lemon, sliced, to serve

Mix together the tamarind sauce (you should
have 200g), agave or sugar, orange blossom water
and the water.

Pour over some ice cubes and add a slice of lemon.

Pictured overleaf.

CHAI

Tea

SERVES 2

2 cardamom pods
½ cinnamon stick
1 teaspoon Earl Grey tea leaves
Sugar (optional)

Add the cardamom, cinnamon and tea to a teapot
and fill with boiling water. Allow to brew for
5 minutes before straining into mugs. Serve
with a little sugar, if you like.

KAMUN

SERVES 2

1 tablespoon cumin seeds
1 lemon

Add the cumin seeds to a teapot and fill with boiling
water. Allow to brew for 5 minutes before straining
into mugs with a squeeze of lemon.

Pictured right.

A FINAL MESSAGE

IF THERE'S ONE MESSAGE I want my story to spread, it's to not take what you have for granted because you don't know when it might be taken from you. How many times in our global history do we have to suffer, how many millions have to die or flee their homes to know that our freedom can be removed so quickly, before we learn to protect it? To hold it close and not let it go?

When life is good, we think it will stay like this forever. But look around you. I'm not a politician, I would never want to be one, but even I can see that when you put money and power first, when you put profits and personal gain over protecting people, you are being short-sighted. It's not how you build a great country it's how you create a temporary win for your party. When you prioritise the people, when you support them, educate them, house them, protect their access to healthcare, you are building a strong nation that will be productive and happy for hundreds of years.

Many people are afraid of refugees, of asylum seekers. Don't be. I'm not saying we are all angels, but not all people are angels either. We are just normal people, forced into situations we never dreamed of. If you want to hear about what it's like to be a refugee, ask them; ask me. I know about these experiences. If you want to know about any minority, just speak to them. Don't listen to the ugly media that make us all out to be bad people. Being a refugee doesn't mean I am less educated, know less about the world, was less successful. And people don't only flee because of war; they are forced to leave their homes because of earthquakes, floods, droughts. Even here in the UK people are starting to feel the consequences of our changing planet. Refugees are like everyone else around you. Let's respect each other because we are all the same, we are all human beings. We don't know what each other has been through to be here today.

When we listen to the lies of our leaders, their repeated corruption and do nothing about it, we lose our power, we lose our voice and often without noticing, bit by bit we lose our liberties. I'm not talking about Syria here; I'm talking about the UK. The British people were told life would be better after Brexit, but it is worse. Far worse than before. Who'd have thought our nurses would be relying on foodbanks, that people cannot afford to heat their homes?

We need to raise up our voices. This is the simplest thing you can do. Help as much as you can. Come together on a human level. Search for charities that support people on the ground. Try to make changes where you can, speak to each other, learn from each other. Vote for change if you don't like what you see.

The world is full of amazing, generous people, there is so much love –
I have seen it first-hand! And if we come together, we can achieve miracles.
We need to feel part of the whole world. We need to get rid of the idea
of some people being better than others. We need to listen to each other,
to not be scared of things we don't know, to learn about one another. We
are a global community now. We are not our governments, and we need
to have a voice. You don't know how important your voice is. I don't think
Ukranians thought that this was possible a few years ago, but now they are
refugees. Don't think it can't happen to you. It happened to me, and it can
happen to everyone.

CONVERSION
CHARTS

LIQUID MEASURES

METRIC	IMPERIAL
1.25ml	¼ tsp
2.5ml	½ tsp
5ml	1 tsp
15ml	1 tbsp
30ml	1fl oz (2 tbsp)
50ml	2fl oz
75ml	3fl oz
100ml	3½fl oz
125ml	4fl oz
150ml	5fl oz (¼ UK pint)
175ml	6fl oz
200ml	7fl oz
250ml	8fl oz
275ml	9fl oz
300ml	10fl oz (½ Imperial pint)
325ml	11fl oz
350ml	12fl oz
375ml	13fl oz
400ml	14fl oz
450ml	15fl oz (¾ pint)
475ml	16fl oz (1 US pint)
500ml	18fl oz
600ml	20fl oz (1 UK pint)
700ml	1¼ pints (25 fl oz)
850ml	1½ pints (30 fl oz)
1 litre	1¾ pints (35 fl oz)
1.2 litres	2 pints (40 fl oz)
1.3 litres	2¼ pints
1.4 litres	2½ pints
1.75 litres	3 pints
2 litres	3½ pints
3 litres	5 pints

SPOONS

1 tsp	5ml
1 dsp	10ml
1 tbsp (3 tsp)	15ml

DRY WEIGHTS

METRIC	IMPERIAL
10g	¼oz
15g	½oz
20g	¾oz
25g	1oz
40g	1½oz
50g	2oz
60g	2¼oz
70g	2¾oz
75g	3oz
100g	3½oz
115g	4oz
125g	4½oz
140g	4¾oz
150g	5oz
160g	5½oz
175g	6oz
200g	7oz
225g	8oz
250g	9oz
275g	9½oz
300g	11oz
350g	12oz
375g	13oz
400g	14oz
425g	15oz
450g	16oz (1lb)
500g (0.5kg)	1lb 2oz
550g	1¼lb
600g	1lb 5oz
675g	1½lb
725g	1lb 10oz
800g	1¾lb
850g	1lb 14oz
900g	2lb
1kg	2¼lb
1.1kg	2½lb
1.25kg	2¾lb
1.3kg	3lb
1.5kg	3¼lb
1.6kg	3½lb
1.8kg	4lb
2kg	4½lb

INDEX

P

parsley
- baby aubergines and cheese 110–111
- biwas 104
- chermoula 105
- daka 105
- fwl mudamis 198
- mtuma (crushed new potatoes) 114–115
- mujadara salad 160–161
- saj 132–133
- tabbouleh 100–101

pasta, angel hair
- plain bulgur 49
- riz shaeiria 48

pasta: haraa asbaeu 130–131
peas: filo rice 194–197

peppers
- Imad's sauce 36
- kabsa rice with chicken 164–165
- kabsa rice with prawns 162–163
- kabsa rice with vegetables 166
- manzilat betinjam 178–179
- moussaka 192–193
- muhammara 94–95
- sahan kudra 44–45
- sawda (lamb's liver) 78–79
- stuffed courgettes, aubergines and peppers 167
- zahraa harra 148–149

pickled cucumbers and chillies 56–57
- falafel wrap 122–123
- mujadara 158–159

pine nuts 17
- filo rice 194–197
- hummus bellahma 74–75
- kabsa rice with chicken 164–165
- kabsa rice with prawns 162–163
- kabsa rice with vegetables 166
- kippeh 182
- kippeh meqlia 183–185
- mujadara salad 160–161

pistachios
- baklawa 204–206
- bird's nest 220–221
- konafa nableseh 230–231
- rolled baklawa 207–209
- tamriah 218–219

pomegranate molasses 17
- biwas 104
- fattoush salad 106–109
- haraa asbaeu 130–131
- kuftah tahini 172–175
- moussaka 192–193
- muhammara 94–95
- sbanakh khudra (green spinach) 112–113
- ylangy (vine leaves) 76–77

pomegranate seeds
- fattoush salad 106–109
- haraa asbaeu 130–131
- muhammara 94–95
- sbanakh khudra (green spinach) 112–113
- tabbouleh 100–101

potatoes
- batata harra 134–135
- jaj bailfurn (grilled chicken thighs) 154–155
- mahashi (stuffed vine leaves) 152–153
- mtuma 114–115
- Syrian fish and chips with tahini sauce 156–157
- ylangy (vine leaves) 76–77

prawns: kabsa rice with prawns 162–163

Q

qawah 238–239

R

radishes
- mujadara salad 160–161
- sahan kudra 44–45

raisins
- kabsa rice with chicken 164–165
- kabsa rice with prawns 162–163
- kabsa rice with vegetables 166

'ready things' 46–47
red taouk 33
refugees 7, 8, 124–127, 168–169, 188, 210–211, 229, 244

rice
- filo rice 194–197
- kabsa rice with chicken 164–165
- kabsa rice with prawns 162–163
- kabsa rice with vegetables 166
- mahashi (stuffed vine leaves) 152–153
- makloubeh 186–187
- riz shaeiria 48
- shurabat ends (lentil soup) 140–141
- stuffed courgettes, aubergines and peppers 167
- types to use 17
- ylangy (vine leaves) 76–77

rocket salad 102–103
rolled baklawa 207–209
Rybak, Stephanie 212

S

sahan kudra 44–45
saj 132–133
saroja 110–111

sauces
- Imad's sauce 36
- shata (chilli sauce) 50–51
- tahini sauce 54

sawda 78–79
sbanakh khudra 112–113
semolina: besbusi 222–225

sesame seeds
- baby aubergines and cheese 110–111
- date and tahini sweet dip 214–215
- dukkah 29
- falafel 116–121

shata 50–51

THANK YOU TO

To my mother and father; my wife, Batool, and my daughters Dana, Lana and Mariam Alarnab.

Heidi Nam Knudsen

Gemma Bell

Gemma Bell and company

Layla Yarjani

Hortense Decaux

Serena Guen

Josephine Naughton

David and Jenny Edington

Jazz Sherman

Asma khan

Hassan Akkad

A H Alaa

A K Amar

Ross Bailey

Philip Khoury

Melissa Hemsley

Imran Khan and family

Farah Bsieso

Alice Aedy

Jay Rayner

HRH Prince El Hassan bin Talal

Mohammed Khaeir Abukalam

Philli Boyle

Joy Said

Amel Hamza

Simon J Quayle

Elisa Dglv

Toni Broodelle

Gerry Pridham

Sahar Pridham

✧ Tom Doust
✧ Vanessa Faulkner
✧ Marlow Refugee Action
✧ Wycombe Refugee Partnership
✧ Emily Madera
✧ Cassy Paris
✧ Choose Love
✧ Appear here
✧ Saima Khan
✧ Airbnb
✧ Kind Snacks
✧ Clerkenwell Boy
✧ Dave Burt
✧ Alice Sampo
✧ Ahmad Algeria
✧ Frederique Bougault
✧ Ahmad Elsidawi
✧ Kate Walsh
✧ Saleema Burney
✧ Tanveer Husain
✧ Stephanie Rybak
✧ Thabet Kalthoum
✧ Daisy Squires
✧ Mohammad Alarnab
✧ Rania Alarnab
✧ The Lady from Norway
✧ who I met in Greece
✧
✧
✧
✧ My agent Rachel Mills, the designers at
✧ Evi-O.Studio, my editor Laura Bayliss,
✧ photographer Andy Sewell, food stylist
✧ Kitty Coles, prop stylist Louie Waller and
✧ all those at HQ and HarperCollins.
✧
✧
✧
✧

HQ
An imprint of HarperCollinsPublishers Ltd
1 London Bridge Street
London SE1 9GF

www.harpercollins.co.uk

HarperCollinsPublishers
Macken House, 39/40 Mayor Street Upper
Dublin 1, D01 C9W8
Ireland

10 9 8 7 6 5 4 3 2

First published
in Great Britain by HQ, an imprint
of HarperCollinsPublishers Ltd 2023

ISBN 978-0-00-853237-6

This book is produced from
independently certified FSC™ paper
to ensure responsible forest management.

For more information visit:
www.harpercollins.co.uk/green

Printed and bound in Bosnia and Herzegovina
by GPS Group.

Design and illustration:
Evi-O.Studio | Susan Le
Illustration Assistants:
Evi-O.Studio | Katherine Zhang & Siena Zadro
Typesetting: Evi-O.Studio | Marcus Cheong
Editor: Laura Bayliss
Photography: Andy Sewell
Food stylist: Kitty Coles
Prop stylist: Louie Waller
Copy-editor: Sally Somers
Art Director: Laura Russell
Publishing Director: Louise McKeever
Production: Halema Begum